Tiger by the Tail

Tiger by the Tail

China and the World Trade Organization

Mark A. Groombridge
and
Claude E. Barfield

The AEI Press

Publisher for the American Enterprise Institute
WASHINGTON, D.C.
1999

To order call toll free 1-800-462-6420 or 1-717-794-3800. For all other inquiries please contact the AEI Press, 1150 Seventeenth Street, N.W., Washington, D.C. 20036 or call 1-800-862-5801.

Library of Congress Cataloging-in-Publication Data

Groombridge. Mark A.
   Tiger by the tail : China and the World Trade Organization / by
Mark A. Groombridge and Claude E. Barfield.
     p.   cm.
Includes index.
ISBN 0-8447-4107-8 (cloth : alk. paper).—ISBN 978-0-8447-4108-6
(pbk. : alk. paper)
   1. World Trade Organization—China. 2. China—Commercial policy.
3. Protectionism—China. 4. China—Foreign economic relations—
United States. 5. United States—Foreign economic relations—
China. I. Barfield. Claude E. II. title.
HF1385.G76   1999
382'.0951073—dc21   99-31188
                                                  CIP

1 3 5 7 9 10 8 6 4 2

The AEI Press
Publisher for the American Enterprise Institute
1150 17th Street, N.W., Washington, D.C. 20036

虎

Contents

—————————— 虎 ——————————

Acknowledgments

Following the twists and turns in the road of China's accession process to the World Trade Organization, particularly in 1999, has been an arduous task. Fortunately, a number of individuals kept us on track through their probing insights and valuable comments. In particular, the authors would like to thank Frederick Abbott, Alan Alexandroff, Judith Bello, Robert Herzstein, Gary Hufbauer, Julius Katz, Patrick Low, Sylvia Ostry, Pitman Potter, Sarath Rajapatirana, and Alan Winters for carefully reading and commenting on the manuscript. James Lilley and Arthur Waldron also provided useful sounding boards for our ideas. All are absolved, of course, from any responsibility for any inadequacies.

The American Enterprise Institute provided an ideal setting for the completion of this book. Of course, institutions do not act, individuals do—and there are a number who deserve our thanks. The authors would first like to thank Chiann Bao, Ingo Fritzen, Seth Harvey, Lu Jiaqing, Moonhui Kim, and Eunsook Kim for their research support. Many others at AEI provided a variety of assistance, including Virginia Bryant, Rebecca Graeves, and MengHao Zhao. We owe a special thanks to our editor, Cheryl Weissman, who more than any other had to follow the tortuous path of China's accession process, given her willingness to reedit chapters so that the book reflects present-day realities.

Finally, our thanks to Carol and Nino at the restaurant Relish, who on many a Friday night had to listen to us debate the issues presented in this book.

Washington, D.C., June 1999

1

虎

Introduction

Prospects for the accession of the People's Republic of China (PRC) to the World Trade Organization (WTO) fluctuated wildly in 1999. At the beginning of the year an accord seemed unlikely, as China was unwilling to make key concessions on market access for foreign firms in such key sectors as telecommunications, financial services, and agriculture. Then, Premier Zhu Rongji took an active role in the negotiations, and the situation looked more auspicious.

The End of Stalemate?

It seemed quite likely that an agreement would be reached during Zhu's visit to the United States in April 1999. Premier Zhu came to the United States with a market-access package that made key concessions on important sectors—concessions that went far beyond those undertaken by many other countries as the price of admission to the multilateral trading system.[1]

At the last moment President Clinton rejected a deal that would have paved the way for China to enter the WTO before the Seattle ministerial meeting at the end of 1999. He was fearful of appearing too soft on China in light of campaign-finance and nuclear-espionage scandals, and domestic interest groups (notably labor unions and the steel and textile industries) were exerting pressure against Chinese membership as well.

Then, in May 1999, two new issues arose, further complicating the process of China's accession. First, NATO's bombing of the Chinese embassy in Belgrade strengthened the hand of the anti-reformists in China, who were also opposed to WTO membership. Second, a much clearer picture emerged of China's nuclear-espionage activities in the United States with the publication of the so-called Cox Report, strengthening the hand of hard-liners in the United States who sought to punish the Chinese by denying them entry into the WTO.

The Argument

This book does not attempt to resolve the long-standing debate on the degree to which national security issues should trump trading relationships between countries.[2] The focus rather is on the economic arguments relating to China's accession to the WTO. Whatever the final outcome, it is now clear that broad market-access terms of accession have been established. But the unexpected and startling events that transpired during the spring of 1999 reinforce the main argument and thesis of this study. It is this: although market-access concessions (tariff reduction and liberalization, particularly in service sectors) are critical to China's bid for WTO membership, the real challenges revolve around "transparency" issues—the legal and administrative policies and apparatus that the PRC must establish to ensure equitable and efficient resolution of commercial and trade disputes. It is the contention of this study that even if substantial portions of the April concessions remain in place, unless China is forced to accept administrative reform as a condition of WTO membership and adopts market-enhancing antidumping and safeguard provisions for responding to import surges, the WTO will face enervating disruptions and turmoil for many years to come after China's accession.

It is true that sectors vary widely in their progress with regard to market forces. For all its reforms, the PRC economy is most accurately labeled a hybrid, combining elements of both central planning and market pricing.[3] But despite the importance of sectoral negotiations, the greatest danger looming is the hypercritical American concern over whether China takes five or eight years to implement the agreement. Such punctiliousness can distract negotiators from focusing on the larger and more important goal of developing transparent institutions in China.

Our concern regarding transparency and administered-protection issues is heightened by the sweeping nature of the package of reforms to which Premier Zhu Rongji agreed, and by our skepticism about the ability of China, even with the best of intentions, to deliver on key elements of any package it offers. Undoubtedly, market liberalization on the scale promised by China will increase the efficiency and productivity of its economy in the long term; but in the short and medium terms, these reforms will force a massive economic overhaul and exert heavy social and political pressure on the government and ruling party. China's Ministry of Labor already expects that the state-welfare system will come under unprecedented attack as the country's ailing state-owned enterprises (SOEs), half of which are losing money, continue to lay off workers. Government officials predict that welfare rolls will expand to some 110 million people by the end of 1999, 26 million more than in 1998.[4]

Moreover, it is clear that powerful political and institutional forces oppose Zhu and other pro-reformers. Zhu himself is only the number-three man in the PRC hierarchy, and while Jiang Zemin has been supportive of economic reform, Li Peng, the number-two man, has been openly resistant to change. A recent statement exemplifying this attitude, widely attributed to a high-ranking government official, bluntly stated, "The grace period [for opening sectors to competition] is in fact just a suspended death sentence before developed countries come to destroy the industries of developing countries."[5]

For these reasons, we argue that the Protocol of Accession for China's WTO membership should include a detailed blueprint for fundamental changes to China's current legal and administrative systems, as well as special procedures for dealing with import surges (antidumping and safeguards actions). The options are clear: either China (and later the other nonmarket economies [NMEs]) agrees to create and implement a rules-based, legally tighter administrative system that commands the respect of the international trading community, or WTO members will establish "managed trade" solutions for China—such as targeted-import quotas and market-share mandates—and, consequently, for other prospective member nations for years to come.

Prior to Zhu's visit, the standoff regarding WTO membership for China had already taken an ominous turn as trade hawks in the United States expressed alarm at the consequences of further delay and began advocating managed-trade solutions. They pointed out that since China need not abide by international trading rules, procrastination would spur an increase in the already enormous U.S. trade deficit with China—which increased twenty-fold after the mid-1980s, to some $58 billion at the end of 1998. If current negotiations fail, the argument goes, the Clinton administration should mount a series of unfair-trade-practice actions against China, forcing it to make further concessions. The United States should "send a strong message to China" with a vigorous invocation of Section 301 suits, asserted Greg Mastel of the Economic Strategy Institute in December 1998.[6] Bruce Stokes, a senior fellow at the Council on Foreign Relations, warned that because of the U.S. political cycle, delaying the issue beyond the spring of 1999 could forestall the possibility of WTO membership for China for some years: "Under the worst-case scenario, if a deal is not struck in early 1999, the next opportunity for China's WTO membership is 2003." Before the April breakthrough, Stokes (like Mastel) had recommended major policy changes and new tactics to jump-start the process—including possible unfair-trade-practice actions and selective increases in tariffs.[7]

Trade hawks contend that the WTO should measure PRC compliance in terms of trade outcomes rather than in terms of the process or procedures by which such trade is conducted. Chalmers Johnson argues as follows:

> How does the United States promote China's economic development while preventing predatory trade from provoking international conflict? The answer is managed trade—using public policy to manage outcomes rather than procedures. . . . Trade management need not seek exact bilateral balances or zero trade deficits. Its criterion should be the health of domestic high-value-added industries—in other words, those that provide technologically advanced jobs for American citizens.[8]

Johnson and others would establish specific quantifiable targets, such as imports or foreign-market shares for particular products. Some analysts argue this case more broadly. One labor-industry coalition, for example, maintains that "although there has been a clear movement away from the use of benchmarks in trade agreements, it is time to reevaluate this trend. The more quantifiable the agreement—the United States-Japan Semiconductor Agreements being a good example—the more likely it can be properly enforced."[9] With regard to China, Mastel observes, "Targets for increased imports would clearly move China in the right direction—toward market opening. This same case was so compelling when made with regard to Poland and Romania thirty-five years ago that Japan and Europe both supported import targets. Let us hope that the wisdom of the past will not be lost on today's decisionmakers."[10]

We believe that the foregoing view can be shown as historically false. Persuasive evidence indicates, for example, that the United States-Japan Semiconductor Agreement was a costly failure for the United States.[11] Mastel's interpretation of the Polish and Romanian General Agreement on Tariffs and Trade (GATT) experiences is flawed as well. Managed trade proved to be unworkable, and it eventually led to years of quota-based protectionism by GATT members against those countries. As Leah Haus points out, "It is extremely difficult, if not impossible, to obtain evidence that would indicate whether contracting parties did indeed obtain increased export opportunities as a result of these entrance fees or whether export opportunities would have been the same, regardless of the Eastern European commitments to the GATT."[12]

In challenging the historical interpretations of the managed traders, we offer radically different, rule-based options both for long-term, market-access commitments and for transition agreements. Building on the civil law exemplified in some European countries (and recently emulated in the United States), we believe that the terms of accession call for major reforms in the Chinese administrative law system. These would include the establishment of special tribunals for foreign economic disputes and the development of fundamental rules for administrative due process.

We offer these recommendations in full awareness of the potential dangers of ambitious "legal transplantation." Western experts who participated in law-and-development programs three decades ago naively trusted that our legal precepts could "socially engineer" broad-based improvements in former colonial countries. The attempt was fraught with hubris. As William Alford has cautioned:

> The ready and frequent use . . . of massive threats to secure changes in the municipal laws of another sovereign state may extract short-term concessions designed chiefly to ease such pressure. . . . It is, however, incapable of generating the type of domestic rationale and conditions needed to produce enduring change. . . . Without a concomitant nurturing of the institutions, personnel, interests, and values capable

of sustaining a liberal, rights-based legality . . . free-standing foreign-derived rules on rarified private property rights, held in significant measure by foreign parties, are, ultimately, of limited utility.[13]

In defense of our recommendations we offer two arguments. First, we do not seek wholesale reform of the body of Chinese administrative law. Rather, we suggest specific reform in the area of foreign economic disputes, where we believe it is possible to persuade the Chinese that their own economic interests will dovetail with those of their foreign economic partners. The second argument is pragmatic: the alternatives advanced so vigorously by trade hawks are unpalatable to, and likely to be rejected by, key interest groups in the emerging foreign-trade and investment sectors in the PRC.

Regarding the potential trade remedies that WTO members could invoke should the PRC not live up to its obligations, there are two sensitive policy areas: dumping and safeguards. Significantly, during the path-breaking negotiations in April, the two sides remained at loggerheads over the details of safeguards and dumping after PRC membership in the WTO; China insisted that there be no separate regimes, and U.S. negotiators demanded open-ended special protections against import surges. We propose, first, transitional mechanisms that would promote and reward market-oriented policies, and second, a timetable for ending any special rules.

Although this is a unique case in many ways, how the world integrates China into the WTO has important implications for other nonmarket economies. Currently there are seventeen NMEs waiting in the wings for WTO membership—Russia, Ukraine, and Vietnam are three of them. The precedents set by the Chinese process will have far-reaching consequences for these countries' terms of accession, for the WTO, and for the future of multilateral trading.

It is important to focus too on the larger picture of building a multilateral trading institution that is truly a *world* trade organization. While not advocating a "get China into the WTO at all costs" position, the authors emphatically maintain that China's membership is important both for China and for the world trading community. Membership will allow China to attain three concrete goals: permanent assurance of nondiscrimination, through most-favored-nation status; insulation against unilateral trade sanctions, through participation in a legally binding dispute-settlement system; and a future voice in establishing new trading rules in such areas as environment, investment, and competition policy. In addition, China's membership in the WTO will help spur the reform effort in that country. Symbolically, membership in the WTO will help integrate China into the world community.

China's accession to the WTO will benefit the world community as well. It will help foreign firms secure access to China's domestic market. It will also secure access for global consumers to inexpensive Chinese imports. More important, it will hinder developed countries (like the United States) from adopting ill-advised, unilateral protectionist policies—such as antidumping provisions.

Plan of the Book

Analysts have addressed the major sources of disagreement in a variety of contexts, but few have attempted to assemble all the pieces of the puzzle. We will do so in the following fashion. In chapter 2 we briefly trace the emergence of China into the world market and analyze the factors behind its trade balance with the world and with the United States. We then describe the evolution and current status of China's WTO-accession negotiations. We also examine the progress (or lack thereof) that has been made in particular sectors in the PRC. Chapter 3 addresses the particular challenges presented by China's mixed economy in light of the experience of other nonmarket economies. Chapter 4 looks at the current stand-off in the negotiations as they relate to trade remedies—that is, antidumping and safeguards—and to transparency. We also present recommendations for rule-based solutions designed to induce market-based, rather than managed-trade, outcomes. In chapter 5 we suggest changes that would invest the current Transition Policy Review Mechanism system with authority over the accession of all transition economies into the WTO. We then summarize our recommendations in concluding remarks.

2

虎

Major Negotiating Issues

Since the launching of the Open Door Policy in 1978, concomitant with the rise to power of Deng Xiaoping, China has emerged as an increasingly important player in the world trading system. The internationalization of the Chinese economy has expanded at a dizzying pace throughout the reform period. In 1978 trade accounted for roughly 10 percent of the country's gross domestic product (GDP). By 1991, however, trade accounted for roughly 28 percent of GDP, and by 1996 the number was closer to 36 percent.[1]

China Enters the World Market

It is important to put these GDP figures into perspective, though, for two reasons. First, there is considerable dispute over the degree to which trade is important to the PRC. When measuring trade as a percentage share of GDP, it should be noted that trade is a gross measure, whereas GDP is a net concept. The distinction is important because trade in China is dominated by the processing of low-value-added imported inputs. Second, considerable evidence suggests that China's GDP was grossly overvalued in the early part of the reform period. This is not surprising, given the considerable price distortions in the PRC that lead different analysts to predict, for example, a GDP per capita range of $350 to $1,200. Astute observers wisely caution that although "trade is important to China . . . what goes on in the rest of its huge economy remains the critical factor."[2]

It is also noteworthy that although China has kept pace interna-

TABLE 2-1
CHINA'S EXPORT SHARE AND RANKING IN WORLD TOTAL EXPORTS,
1980-1996
(value unit: $U.S. million)

Year	World Exports	China Exports	China's Share (percentage)	Ranking
1980	1,990,568	18,119	0.9	26
1981	1,972,439	22,007	1.1	19
1982	1,830,835	22,321	1.2	17
1983	1,807,844	22,226	1.2	17
1984	1,901,873	26,139	1.4	18
1985	1,927,707	27,350	1.4	17
1986	2,115,696	30,942	1.5	16
1987	2,496,878	39,437	1.6	16
1988	2,838,223	47,516	1.7	16
1989	3,036,065	52,538	1.7	14
1990	3,470,000	62,093	1.8	15
1991	3,530,000	71,842	2.0	13
1992	3,700,000	84,940	2.3	11
1993	3,687,000	91,763	2.5	11
1994	4,168,300	121,038	2.9	11
1995	5,020,000	148,770	3.0	11
1996	5,254,000	151,066	2.9	11

SOURCE: *Almanac of China's Foreign Economic Relations and Trade 1997–1998* (Beijing: China National Economy Publishing House, September 1997), p. 456.

tionally in recent years in share of world exports, it still accounts for only a small percentage of total world trade. As table 2–1 indicates, China was responsible for about 3 percent of the world's export trade in the 1990s.

This is by no means to discount, however, the growing role that Chinese exports have played in contributing to the health of the economy. Chinese government officials routinely note that export growth has been responsible for about 20 percent of China's GDP growth throughout the reform period.[3] And it is certainly true that export growth in China has exploded. Table 2–2 documents this growth.

The U.S. Policy Response: The Trade Deficit Scapegoat

Ironically, it is China's surge in exports that has hindered its entry into the WTO, largely because of U.S. paranoia and misunderstanding

TABLE 2–2
CHINA'S WORLD TRADE, 1978–1997
(\$U.S. billions)

Year	1978	1979	1980	1981	1982	1983	1984	1985	1986	1987	1988	1989	1990	1991	1992	1993	1994	1995	1996	1997
Exports	9.75	13.66	18.12	22.01	22.32	22.23	26.14	27.35	30.94	39.44	47.52	52.54	62.09	71.84	84.94	91.74	121.04	148.78	151.06	182.7
%		28.6	24.6	17.7	1.4	-0.4	15.0	4.4	11.6	21.6	17.0	9.6	15.4	13.6	15.4	7.4	24.2	18.6	1.5	17.3
Imports	10.89	15.67	20.02	22.02	19.29	21.39	27.41	42.25	42.9	43.22	55.28	59.14	53.35	63.79	80.59	103.96	115.69	132.08	138.84	142.4
%		30.5	21.7	9.1	-14.2	9.8	22.0	35.1	1.5	0.7	21.8	6.5	-10.9	16.4	20.8	22.5	10.1	12.4	4.9	2.5
Total	20.64	29.33	38.14	44.03	41.61	43.62	53.55	69.6	73.84	82.66	102.8	111.68	115.44	135.63	165.53	195.7	236.73	280.86	289.9	325.1

SOURCES: *China Statistical Yearbook*, various years, and United States–China Business Council.

over the bilateral trade deficit. We recognize that the United States must overcome significant hurdles if our recommendations are to be adopted. First, we need to persuade U.S. authorities to stop formulating policy according to trade account figures. Currently, the United States is believed to have close to a $70 billion trade deficit with China. It is likely that this number will continue to increase, given the economic crisis afflicting Asia.[4] Government officials from the United States routinely complain, "We can't allow that to continue. It hurts us economically, and it won't lead to China's ability to accede to the World Trade Organization."[5] In September 1998, for example, one U.S. official remarked, "We recognize that the Chinese have lots of difficult problems to face. . . . But my job is to make sure that on that list of problems is this trade deficit and the treatment of businesses here [China]."[6]

The U.S. leadership's viewpoint may well reflect political reality, but it is based on a woeful ignorance of basic economic theory. It also reflects a misunderstanding of the facts specific to the United States-China bilateral trading relationship. On the broader level, the vast literature of economic theory suggests that trade deficits matter very little to the economic health of a country. The trade deficit (or surplus) is a reflection of the *current account*, which records all trade in merchandise goods and services. Conversely, the *capital account* records all trade in assets, including portfolio or direct investments. As economists routinely note, "The magnitude of the account deficit or surplus is determined by a country's savings-investment ratio. By definition, a country's current account balance equals its excess of saving over investment: when saving exceeds investment, the current account is positive, and domestic residents are acquiring foreign assets."[7] It ill behooves us to blame the lender who tides U.S. citizens over in this situation. For this reason, Douglas Irwin, speaking for most international trade economists, notes that a "country's trade balance is related to international capital flows—not to open or closed markets, unfair trade practices, or national competitiveness." Unfortunately, though, "this lesson is still apparently lost on many policy officials today."[8]

It is also important to examine the specifics of the bilateral trading relationship between the United States and China. First, it is inevitable that countries will run deficits with some countries and surpluses with others, even if their total trade is balanced. In the case of China, though, there are wildly divergent reports as to the actual amount of the deficit. For example, in 1997 the United States estimated that it had a $49.7 billion trade deficit with China, while China estimated only $16.3 billion. In 1998, the United States reported a bilateral trade deficit with China of some $60 billion, while China said the number was closer to $23 billion.

Regardless of the discrepancy, it is noteworthy that the United States has traditionally adopted a double standard with regard to imports and exports from Hong Kong. Exports from the United States destined for China that are distributed by middlemen in Hong Kong are counted as exports to Hong Kong, whereas imports into the United States from China handled by Hong Kong middlemen are counted as imports from China. For this reason, in agreement with Nicholas Lardy, we argue that "U.S. data on bilateral trade with China are seriously flawed," and that "the argument that the growing deficit with China has caused a large loss of manufacturing jobs in the United States is wrong."[9] The reason is straightforward: investors in a number of countries, largely from East and Southeast Asia, have relocated production facilities to the People's Republic of China. Consequently, the growth in the bilateral trade deficit with China is not nearly as dramatic as some might think, because job opportunities taken away by China were transferred to other countries one or two decades ago.[10]

Finally, with regard to the trade deficit, it is important to note the composition of goods traded between China and the United States. As figures 2–1 and 2–2 suggest, goods imported into the United States from China fall almost entirely into the category of sectors where the United States is increasingly noncompetitive. Conversely, the products that the United States exports to China reflect our comparative advantage in high technology and knowledge-based industries. For this reason, we believe that the United States should drop its demand for extended protection of textiles and apparel. U.S. competitiveness is not likely to be enhanced by protecting these noncompetitive sectors here at home.

A History of the Chinese GATT and WTO Negotiating Process

When the General Agreement on Tariffs and Trade (GATT) was founded in 1948, China was one of the founding members. It was not clear, however, *which* China that was. After losing the civil war to the Chinese Communist Party (CCP) in 1949, the Nationalist Party (*Kuomindang*, or KMD) fled to Taiwan and established the Republic

FIGURE 2–1
TOP TEN U.S. IMPORTS FROM CHINA AS A PERCENTAGE OF TOTAL
U.S. IMPORTS FROM CHINA, 1997

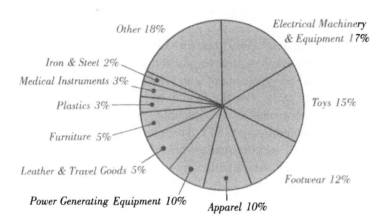

SOURCE: U.S. Department of Commerce. Reprinted by United States-China Business
Council. Website: www.uschina.org

FIGURE 2–2
TOP TEN U.S. EXPORTS TO CHINA AS A PERCENTAGE OF TOTAL
U.S. EXPORTS TO CHINA, 1997

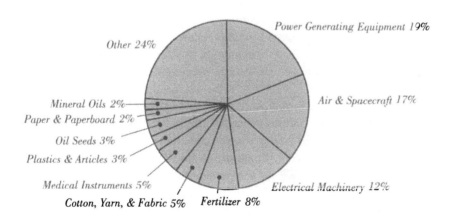

SOURCE: U.S. Department of Commerce. Reprinted by United States-China Business
Council. Website: www.uschina.org

of China (ROC). The ROC on Taiwan remained a member of the GATT immediately after losing the civil war, but withdrew in 1950. Given the political climate at the time, there was little support for bringing the PRC into the GATT. In 1965 the ROC gained observer status to the GATT, but it lost this status when the PRC joined the United Nations in 1971.

It was not until July 1986 that the PRC sent a delegation to Geneva to submit a formal request to join the GATT.[11] This is not to say that the PRC had no involvement with GATT prior to formal application. In 1980, two years after the launch of the Open Door Policy, the PRC began sending officials to economic, trade, and commercial policy courses conducted by the GATT. These early signals of an interest in joining the GATT were formalized in July 1981, when the PRC requested and received permission to serve as an observer at a GATT meeting on the renewal of the Multifibre Arrangement (MFA), which established rules governing trade in textiles.

Just over one year later, in November 1982, the PRC requested and received permission to serve as an observer on the ministerial session that drew up the priorities for GATT in the 1980s. In December 1983 the PRC applied and was accepted for membership in the MFA. As Harold Jacobson and Michael Oksenberg note, "China decided to participate in MFA because it wanted assurance that the arrangement provides that its growing textile exports would have access to markets in industrialized countries. In addition, participating in MFA would give China experience with GATT procedures."[12] In 1984 the PRC also served as an observer to the GATT proceedings at large. Unfortunately, this observer-status experience was of little use to China as a stepping stone, because of problems inherent to the MFA agreement and because the country remained outside of GATT rules and principles.[13]

In May 1987 a formal working party was established to determine the exact terms and conditions under which the PRC would be allowed to enter the GATT. This step would have been taken sooner but for an initial disagreement over the nature of the PRC's membership: would it be entering the GATT as a new contracting party, or would it be resuming a membership originally established in 1948? The PRC originally claimed, "The founding of the People's Republic of China in 1949 did not alter China's status as a subject of international law. The withdrawal from GATT in 1950 by the deposed regime in Taiwan was illegal and invalid. . . . Therefore, there is a sufficient political and legal basis for China's request for resumption of its status as a contracting party."[14]

Unfortunately, from the perspective of the Chinese, this option of joining the WTO as an original member of the GATT expired as of January 1, 1997. Moreover, had China "resumed" its contracting status, even the Chinese acknowledged that the PRC would have had "to enter into substantive negotiations to set its rights and obligations on the basis of contemporary conditions."[15]

So far, however, thirteen years of negotiation have failed to resolve several thorny issues. Fundamentally, many analysts wonder whether China has sufficiently evolved as a market economy to join the WTO system without irreparably harming that system. In the past thirteen years, more than twenty sessions of the working party have been held, and China has entered into bilateral negotiations with some twenty current WTO members.

The GATT Membership Process

The procedure for entering the GATT is both simple and open-ended. Article XII states merely that a party who is not a member of the GATT may accede to the agreement on terms and conditions to be agreed on between WTO members and the government of the applicant nation. A WTO member may be either a "(sovereign) state or a separate customs territory possessing full autonomy in the conduct of its external commercial relations."[16] Decisions on membership are taken by a two-thirds majority, though in practice achieving a consensus is the real test. Important trading states such as the United States or the European Union can effectively exercise a veto by themselves.

Three documents make up the accession instrument: the *Protocol*, which sets out the terms and conditions for compliance with the general agreement; the report of the *working party*; and the *tariff schedule* and *market-access schedules*, which consist of the bound items of the new member's tariff schedule and individual market-access agreements. The first substantive step toward membership consists of a memorandum from the applicant describing all laws, regulations, and policies affecting trade and investment. At this point the process divides into two tracks. The WTO General Council appoints a working party comprising trade negotiators from WTO members to bargain with the applicant over bringing its domestic laws and regulations into compliance with the WTO. At the end of the process, the working party produces a report that includes "commitment para-graphs" that track the Protocol and are enforceable through the WTO dispute-settlement process. The report also contains a description of the applicant's trade regime, an amplification of the applicant's plan for implementation, and views of working-party members regarding their understanding of the applicant's commitments. As explained by Jeffrey Gertler, a member of the working party on China's accession, this aspect of the Protocol is multilateral in that it establishes how China and WTO members can ensure that China "will have the capac-ity to observe the rules and obligations of the WTO and also to enforce these rules domestically in a uniform and predictable manner, so that foreign businesses and traders are not discriminated against in their operations in China."[17]

At the same time, the potential new member-state undertakes a series of bilateral negotiations with individual WTO members on reciprocal tariff reductions and—of equal importance in recent years—other market-access issues covering agriculture, industrial goods, and services. After the successful conclusion of the bilateral discussions, the working party may submit an accession Protocol for approval by the WTO's top governing body, the ministerial confer-ence. As Gertler continues, "Once China accedes, the results of these bilateral negotiations will be 'multilateralized,' or in other words, they will be extended to all WTO Members on a most-favored-nation basis."

Broader Issues

Let us turn to some of the overarching issues that influence the acces-sion process, which negotiators in the working party are currently ad-dressing. The discussion here is not meant to be exhaustive, and several issues are not dealt with in detail. For example, domestic legal issues in the United States are important, particularly Title IV of the Trade Act of 1974 (also known as Jackson-Vanik) and the Uruguay Round Agreement Act of 1995, which implements the GATT, 1994, in U.S. domestic law. The combination of these two laws makes it possible for the U.S. Congress to hamper China's entry into the WTO. The specific issue concerns the relationship between U.S. domestic law and the GATT agreement. According to Article I of the GATT agreement, countries must grant unconditional, permanent most-fa-vored-nation (MFN) status to all contracting parties or forgo the benefits negotiated in the accession agreement. MFN, often a misunderstood concept in the United States, merely confers normal trade status on a trading partner through nondiscriminatory treatment. (Indeed, recently the term *MFN* was changed to *normal trade relations* [*NTR*] to avoid confusion.) Under Jackson-Vanik, however, the United States reaffirmed a legal ban on granting MFN to countries with "non-market economies" (with the exception of Poland and Yugoslavia). This law was an extension of the Trade Agreements Extension Act of 1951, signed during the Truman administration. When the U.S. Congress ratified the agreements stipulated during the Uruguay Round, it specifically assigned itself a role before permanent MFN could be granted to China. Clearly, as Alan Alexandroff notes, the U.S. Congress intended "to ensure that approval of a new member of the WTO would occur without superseding extant federal legislation."[18] If negotiations for China's accession succeed, congressional leaders plan to have an up or down vote to repeal Jackson-Vanik as far as China is concerned.

These legal matters are important because a host of noneconomic factors could well influence congressional votes. The authors are acutely aware that other issues (such as human rights) influence the U.S. position on China's accession to the WTO. Minority Leader Richard Gephardt, for example, has made it clear that "membership in the WTO involves more than just their economic behavior and their economic relationships."[19] Similarly, we have noticed that recent allegations of Chinese financial contributions to the Democratic Party have had a deleterious effect on China's prospects for entering the WTO. Unhappily, the authors concur with Bruce Stokes in his observation that "the White House's vulnerability on questions of ethics and the GOP's passion for campaign demagoguery could create a combustive political mix with consequences for China policy."[20]

Is the PRC a Developing or Developed Country? Since June 1997, the focus of the talks has shifted from rule-related issues such as nondiscrimination and transparency to specific market-access schedules. Still, one of the broadest issues that confronts the WTO working party is the assessment of whether the PRC is a "developing" or a "developed" country. WTO members that are accorded developing-country status have fewer burdens and responsibilities than have developed or nondeveloping members. Not surprisingly, the PRC contends that it is still a developing country, and thus in need of relaxed terms for accession.

The classification judgment is not a trivial matter. In the Uruguay Round, for example, an agreement was reached on agriculture whereby developed countries were obligated to reduce tariffs on agricultural products by 36 percent over a six-year period, and developing countries were required to reduce them by only 24 percent over a ten-year period. Developing countries also receive a variety of other benefits, such as technical assistance to help develop market-based institutions compatible with WTO rules.

In the Uruguay Round, notably, South Korea, Hong Kong, Singapore, and Malaysia all classified themselves as developing countries in terms of certain market-access negotiations, a point not lost on the PRC. The problem with such a vast and diverse country as the PRC, however, is the mixture of evidence as to its developing or nondeveloping status. Clearly, some sectors and some geographic regions are much more developed than others. A report published in late 1998 by a state-run think tank, the Chinese Academy of Social Sciences (CASS), noted that 70 percent of labor allocation, 62 percent of product pricing and distribution, 51 percent of enterprise management, 23 percent of land transfers, and 17 percent of capital distribution were market-based.[21] Moreover, the PRC has long pursued what it calls a pillar-industry (*zhizhu gongye*) strategy, whereby state leaders extend selective benefits to certain industrial sectors in order to make them more competitive. (The success of this strategy is dubious at best, as we discuss below.)

In light of such policies, of course, some of the sectors are more "advanced" than others. But if the state were to revoke its preferential policies toward such industries, they would not be nearly as competitive. Serious distortions and imbalances currently exist in several former pillar industries, such as textiles, which the state promoted between 1979 and 1988. Since the selective benefits were revoked in response to massive overcapacity, the state has adopted policies that forcibly reduce the number of spindles in operation.[22]

Some geographic regions in the PRC are clearly more advanced than others. The provinces along the eastern seaboard, for example, are much more developed than are the inner provinces. To an extent this regional disparity reflects natural conditions (like access to waterway-transportation networks), but in general it is a function of state policy. Special economic zones (SEZs) were deliberately established along the coast. As Dorothy Solinger notes:

> The policies for the coast—beginning with Guangdong and Fujian provinces' fixed revenue retention rates in 1980 and the creation of four SEZs in these provinces in the same year—entailed a package of tax incentives, reduced tariffs, diminished bureaucracy, licensing priorities, preferential credit policies, price-setting powers, freedom from export duties for finished products, export earnings retention rights, and raw material and capital goods import duty privileges. . . . [And], as it turned out, these privileges were granted [them] not just before, but sometimes also at the expense of, the remaining regions of the country.[23]

In the past few years Beijing has attempted to build up the inland provinces, many of which remain jealous of the formerly privileged coastal provinces. It is common to read that "state preferential policies are now being extended to the hinterland, and the increasing equality of national treatment has consequently weakened policy privileges in coastal areas."[24] Moreover, regardless of policy edicts at the national level, local governments are apparently successful at using extrabudgetary funds to offer preferential policies to outside investors and local firms.[25] Indeed, all thirty provinces in the PRC and thousands of counties and townships have launched their own zones. And regardless of legality, by early 1993 there were some 1,800 zones—including special economic zones, economic development zones, economic and technology development zones—at and above the county level, many of which were not sanctioned by the state and operate illegally.[26] Not surprisingly, the bureaucrats in the legally sanctioned zones resent the competitive challenge created by those in the unofficial zones, whose preferential policies often include the reduction of land prices to levels called "incredible."[27] The net effect of these policies, according to the World Bank, is that China "is in the process of moving away from a system of regional variations in economic incentives, particularly from those which have favored the coastal provinces." Instead the movement is toward "sectoral incentives, regardless of location."[28]

Despite this state policy goal of leveling the playing field among regions, the coastal areas are far outpacing the inland provinces. This is evidenced by the millions of people who are flocking eastward. Moreover, it is difficult for state leaders to mandate the locations where foreigners will invest, and the bulk of foreign money still flows to southern coastal provinces. As K.C. Fung et al. note, "Despite efforts by the Chinese government to diversify the locations of foreign direct investment and despite attempts to lure foreign direct investment inland and towards the western regions, an overwhelming fraction of the foreign direct investment is still concentrated in a handful of regions in the south along the coastal regions of China."[29]

There are yet more issues involved in determining the degree to which the PRC is a developed rather than a developing country. Those claiming that it is a developed country often point out that it is now the world's seventh largest national economy (bolstered by the return of Hong Kong) and tenth largest trading partner. Conversely, PRC officials routinely note that the country has a very low per capita income and that its share of exports on the world market is only about 3 percent. Of course, these statistics vary greatly, depending on whom you ask. Per capita GDP calculations, for example, range from $350 to $1,200. Moreover, it is difficult to measure the meaning of such a number by looking at the purchasing power parity (PPP) of PRC citizens, given price distortions within the economy. Housing costs, for example, are still quite low for close to 90 percent of the urban population, because people are given massive subsidies by the state.

Ultimately, it appears likely and judicious that the WTO will adopt a compromise solution that would avoid placing the PRC in either category exclusively. Already the negotiations on its accession have moved to a sector-by-sector stage. A note of caution is in order, however, as certain sectors might become artificially competitive or advanced as a consequence of state policy. The issue of geographic limitations is more complicated. PRC officials have offered greater market access for telecommunications, for example, in some provinces than in others. Officials rationalize that a uniformity of laws would hinder further liberalization, given the high degree of regional disparities. Outside observers object to this practice, noting that uniformity of laws is a crucial underpinning of the GATT agreement and exceptions to the rule should be rare. But we believe that an accession agreement could certainly accommodate the PRC and allow it to implement different liberalization timetables for different regions.

Transparency and Judicial Review. We will return to the subject of the uniformity of laws in our discussion of the transition mechanism in chapters 4 and 5. Another broad issue to consider here, however, is the nature of the legal system in the PRC. A basic prerequisite for securing effective access to a country's market is an understanding of the rules and regulations that dictate access. Such knowledge often falls under the broader rubric of *transparency*, which refers to "being able to know what that law is and that it will be enforced according to its terms."[30] This leads to the question, To what degree is there an institutional framework to support the enforcement of procedures, rules, regulations? In disseminating knowledge about laws and in enforcing them, the PRC is remiss; but again, this varies greatly across sectors and regions. Even in broad areas such as leadership accession there is arbitrariness, as demonstrated by the purges of Zhao Ziyang in 1989 and Qiao Shi in 1998.[31]

Well before the founding of the People's Republic in October 1949, China embraced legal and administrative traditions very different from those of the West. Throughout China's history there has been a strong tradition of subordinating law to policy—using the law as a means of achieving the goals of the state. It is noteworthy that there is no distinction in the Chinese language between *rule of law* and *rule by law*—both are translated as *fazhi*. In a rule-of-law system, the state and the party (even the Communist Party) would be subject to the same laws. In a rule-by-law system, the law is an instrument to be used by the state to achieve its leadership's goals.

For our purposes, the evolution of commercial contract law is the most important symbol and metaphor for the conflict between rule by law and rule of law. In a recent study, Pitman Potter has analyzed the workings and progress of contract law in China since the passage of the Economic Contract Law (ECL) in 1981. He posits that the ECL is the "cornerstone of the regulatory framework for the economic reforms that emerged [after 1978]."[32] Since the "imposition" of the ECL on the preexisting system in 1981, China has witnessed a struggle at many levels to achieve legitimacy and autonomy for agricultural, commercial, and industrial contracts. As Potter observes, "The function of contracts in the Chinese economy is inextricably tied to the policy issue of whether economic conduct should be based on collectivist central planning or upon more autonomous market-oriented decision making by economic actors themselves."[33]

Both traditional Chinese rules and the socialist law of the PRC "reflected the primacy of the collectivist norms . . . that require[d] contract relations to be subjugated to factors external to the transaction."[34] Over the past two decades there has been a complex interaction among the central leadership, the often skeptical bureaucracy, the new commercial class, and the emerging legal community. The combination of these forces has led to a gradual but uneven advance toward more autonomous contract law. Cautiously optimistic, Potter concludes that the immediate future will present a mixed picture. "Disparities between doctrinal norms and operational reality suggest the effect of preexisting collectivist norms remains strong," he notes. But he goes on to say,

> The practical legitimacy of the ECL will not be an all-or-nothing matter, but rather will be selectively limited to those provisions of the ECL where consistency of doctrine and practice have encouraged practical legitimacy. . . . Economic actors will use contracts to express reciprocal obligations related to their increasingly varied transactions, but will accept certain degrees of external intrusion from personal and organizational relationships. . . . Contract parties will increasingly rely on courts and compulsory dispute resolution to assert their contract rights, but will accept nonmonetary remedies. . . . The autonomy encouraged by legitimation of certain provisions of the ECL is potentially an important precursor to expansion of autonomy in other sectors of Chinese life.[35]

Despite the proliferation of these laws, the attitudes of the officials who enforce these laws are significant. Local bureaucrats exercise de facto property rights over the assets of subordinate enterprises under their jurisdiction.[36] David Granick argues that "decentralization within the Chinese state sector takes the form of regional governments constraining central decisionmaking via their recognized property rights, rather than its occurring through the Center's granting power to lower bodies so as to best achieve the Center's own goals, whether these be efficiency or political objectives."[37]

Sometimes bureaucrats show their power by ignoring central decrees. In the reform era, local-level bureaucrats have their own basis of power and serve as their own watchdogs; hence it is difficult for central leaders to control them. As Premier Zhu often laments, "resistance to the principles, policies, and measures of the central authorities is not weak, which makes it very difficult to implement them. Some party and government chiefs do not feel obliged to listen to the central authorities."[38]

At other times, however, this bureaucratic control over property rights leads to what Jean Oi calls an "entrepreneurial basis of cadre power," which extends well beyond the mere controlling of inputs.[39] As a consequence, bureaucrats often act unilaterally, adopting legislation that is most favorable to them regardless of the effect for the national economy. As one state official has observed, "There is one current problem with legislation. Since the law is drafted and enacted by the responsible department, the responsible department will tend to pass into law what is beneficial to it."[40] In other cases, the ministerial bureaucrats with responsibility for specific industries attempt to exercise control as well. The result, as a state official observed in the *Chinese Legal Daily*, is that "where there are still various government departments in charge of various industries, the market bears a pronounced departmental color and is separated and controlled by the various departments."[41]

Wisely, the PRC announced in September 1998 that it was revising the Regulations on the Reconsideration of Administrative Decisions adopted in 1990.[42] Moreover, it should be noted that the lack of compliance by lower-level bureaucrats is not necessarily deleterious to the economic environment. At times, bureaucrats are able to grease the wheel, approving projects rapidly. And at times the lack of compliance is beneficial for foreign companies, which in some cases would have to deal with dozens of layers of bureaucracy and red tape.

The problem is the arbitrary nature of this bureaucratic malfeasance. Not surprisingly, some bureaucratic interventions take on a more malevolent form: that is, the unproductive seeking of rents and corruption. Officers of the state take kickbacks or engage in outright bribery to issue licenses and permits. One PRC economist estimated in 1993 that the annual net industrial revenue lost to such activities topped 100 billion yuan ($U.S. 8.3 billion).[43] Moreover, other bureaucrats illegally sell state assets. Although exact figures on this abuse are unavailable, the State Assets Management Bureau estimates that losses between 1982 and 1992 came to some 500 billion yuan ($U.S. 60 billion). The bureau notes too that the problem is increasing, because corrupt bureaucrats and company chiefs are abusing their power to obtain at little or no cost the equity stakes in state-owned enterprises (SOEs) undergoing transformation into shareholding companies.[44]

State-Owned Enterprises. A third issue that plays a prominent role in China's accession to the WTO concerns the role of state-owned enterprises and state trading companies. Officially the GATT does not speak directly to the question of ownership. It does, however, discuss how SOEs and state trading companies should be regulated. Article XVII of the GATT and Commercial Considerations Clause states:

> [State Enterprises shall . . . make purchases and sales] solely in accordance with commercial considerations, including price, quality, availability, marketability, transportation and other conditions of purchases or sale, and shall afford the enterprises of the other contracting parties adequate opportunity, in accordance with customary business practice, to compete for participation in such purchases or sales.[45]

With regard to state trading enterprises, one common feature of nonmarket economies is the monopolization by the state of foreign trade transactions. Many firms in countries such as the PRC formerly lacked the autonomy to import or export products on their own. Instead, they were obliged to deal with a separate, state-owned entity that oversaw the process. Similarly, foreign companies could not deal directly with the managers of firms who wished to import inputs; instead, foreign companies had to deal with state-run trading enterprises. Although devolution of trading rights has progressed since the reform period began in 1978, state-run foreign trading companies (FTCs) still accounted for roughly 92 percent of ordinary trade exports in 1995.[46] As one report notes, "China was much slower initially to give direct trading rights to enterprises. There were only a handful with such rights in the mid-1980s, rising to 600 in 1991, and 1,360 in 1993. This number has reportedly risen to over 8,000 in 1995."[47] Ironically, despite the argument that these FTCs are still state controlled, the massive proliferation of such firms makes it very difficult for the central government to control actual volumes of trade.

The primary concern of foreign companies, though, has been the degree to which state-owned FTCs *are the only firms* that can handle imports and exports in the PRC. In the market-access package advanced in April 1999, China made considerable efforts to extend trading and distribution rights to foreign firms. The U.S. Trade Representative (USTR) press release observed that "the United States has sought and won agreement for elimination of these restrictions. China will provide, for the first time, full trading rights and distribution rights to U.S. firms. These will be progressively phased in over three years. Even for its most sensitive and protected industries, such as chemical fertilizers, crude oil, and processed petroleum, China will provide for trading rights and distribution."[48] It remains to be seen how far trading rights in these sensitive sectors will be extended. Managers of oil SOEs in China possess considerable influence over state policymaking. As of this writing, it is not clear whether Premier Zhu consulted with the heads of these sectors before making such significant concessions. The attempted resignation of at least one official (Wu Jichuan, minister of information industries) following Zhu's visit suggests that he did not consult with them.

Foreign buyers of Chinese exports have also seen welcome liberalizing reforms implemented in recent years. One positive step in liberalizing China's trade regime was the announcement in early 1999 that twenty private enterprises would be allowed to import and export freely. These companies, with registered capital of 1.36 billion yuan ($U.S. 164 million), would be engaged in such industries as animal feed, foodstuffs, agricultural development, medicines, metallurgy, construction materials, textiles, garment manufacture and retailing, light industry, electronics and machinery, and computer software development.[49] Other firms in China, notably SOEs, will receive broader trading rights as well. As the United States-China Business Council explains, "Within three years of WTO accession, China has committed to extend general trading rights (import and export) to all companies for all commodities except those explicitly listed in an annex to the Protocol."[50] It should come as little surprise that those excluded commodities include key products in agriculture and other industries dominated by powerful oligopolies, such as chemical fertilizers and crude oil.

Undoubtedly, the progress made on this front stemmed not only from external pressure; throughout the reform period, industrial actors in SOEs exerted strong domestic pressure, as they were constrained from engaging in profitable trading activities. As far back as 1979, for example, players in the steel industry argued,

> The State should grant some rights to factories, mines and other enterprises so that they can engage in foreign trade and economic exchange with foreign countries; it should quickly change the situation in which foreign trade work is put under tight control and good opportunities to earn large

sums of foreign exchange are lost. . . . Granting enterprises some decisionmaking rights in conducting foreign trade and arranging their production will bring about economic results benefiting the State, enterprises and the people.[51]

Considerable debate will persist, though, with regard to the proper role of FTCs in China. In a survey of old-style FTCs in agriculture and minerals, for example, Will Martin and Christian Bach concluded that some of these enterprises "are frequently not transparent in their operation, frequently create vested interests, and fail to achieve their objectives."[52] Newer, more profit-oriented FTCs will likely have to increase their competitiveness as market-oriented reforms in China deepen, but the willingness of state leaders to allow them to go bankrupt is open to question. China's accession to the WTO may help in this regard, as GATT regulations dictate that state-owned trading companies must report their activities to the WTO's Council on Trade in Goods, which is designed to evaluate whether these types of enterprises operate according to "commercial" considerations.

The role of generic state-owned enterprises (as opposed to state trading companies) is more complex. Based on the visit by Zhu Rongji to Washington in April 1999, there appears to be some progress on the issue of SOE reform. According to the U.S. Trade Representative (USTR) press release after Zhu's visit,

China has agreed that it will ensure that state-owned and state-invested enterprises will: make purchases and sales based solely on commercial considerations, such as price, quality, availability and marketability; provide U.S. firms with the opportunity to compete for sales and purchases on nondiscriminatory terms and conditions. China has also agreed that it will not influence these commercial decisions (either directly or indirectly) except in a WTO consistent manner.[53]

Despite this promise by China—or the perception of a promise by USTR officials—the authors consider it naïve to think that China will allow SOEs to make decisions based solely on commercial considerations. China has been attempting to restructure its SOEs since 1978, making the attempt a top priority since 1984. Although considerable progress has been made in some cases, it is clear that commercial factors are not the only considerations; political, social, and dubious economic factors count as well. Politically, some Chinese leaders still see SOEs as a tool to protect state leaders from hostile domestic and foreign forces by preserving control over strategic resources. This certainly applied to the case of the PRC in the mid-1950s;[54] some would argue that it applies to the modern era as well. As one foreign official argues, PRC leaders "are very reluctant to relax their tight grip on what are the core strategic industrial sectors. They don't want to end up like many countries in Africa, where the key natural resources are virtually controlled by multinationals and foreign banks."[55]

With regard to social justifications, it is well recognized that SOEs in China function as the social safety net for much of the citizenry. Many large SOEs maintain day-care centers, kindergartens, elementary and middle schools, universities, stores, post offices, and local police stations. The connections are tenuous in many cases between these divisions and local government, because of the lengthy distance between the SOE and the administrative offices of local authorities.[56] The result, as one of the drafters of the new "company law" joked, is that "only after the cremation do state enterprises stop providing services for individuals."[57] Many SOEs also offer generous retirement and pension packages under the system of retiring on full or near-full pay (*lituixi*). Given the heavy recruitment into the industrial labor force during the 1950s, the fact that large numbers of workers reached retirement age in the 1980s and 1990s was to be expected. Consequently, for many SOEs the ratio of retirees to workers has become 1 to 2; some older SOEs have a ratio of 1 to 1.[58]

Social welfare payments skyrocketed as well from 67 million yuan ($US 8.4 million) in 1978 to 770 million yuan ($US 96.2 million) in 1990, and they are certain to increase in the future.[59] The bulk of this increase came from retirement benefits that accounted for 21.1 percent of total social welfare expenditures in 1978 and jumped to 39.7 percent in 1990.[60] SOEs also subsidize underemployment; reports claim that 25 to 30 percent of the workers are superfluous, working in "empty shell enterprises" (*kongqiao qiye*).[61] Undoubtedly, casting aside these workers raised the specter of social instability, and PRC scholars acknowledge that property rights are delineated with social welfare considerations in mind.[62] For this reason it is common to hear PRC commentators remark that "if we de-nationalize or privatize state-owned enterprises, we will not only wreck the framework of the national economy, but also deprive more than 100 million staff and workers of guarantees covering their livelihood and social insurance benefits. This would certainly be an extremely large factor, tending toward social instability."[63]

On an economic level, Chinese state leaders contend that SOEs supply goods and services that the private sector is either unwilling or unable to provide through the regulation of the market-price mechanism.[64] Whether this is true is debatable, but many believe it is and justify state intervention on the grounds that it protects "infant" and high-tech industries. As we discuss in greater detail below, Chinese leaders advance this argument in the case of telecommunications and other financial services. For many industries, however, it is common to hear economists from state-run think tanks argue that "many of China's industries are still in [their] infancy; therefore it is reasonable to ask for a transition period [in phasing out support]."[65]

Empirically, it is noteworthy too that 2.5 percent of the total SOEs contributed some 60 percent of the profit and tax remittances to state coffers and accounted for 45.6 percent of the country's gross-value industrial output.[66] It is to these large SOEs that state actors refer in the Ninth Five-Year Plan,[67] when they propose to have only 1,000 SOEs serve as the foundation of the national economy under the "big-corporation, big-group" philosophy.[68] One report suggested that the largest 800 of these SOEs already accounted for 63 percent of the fixed capital of industrial SOEs and contributed 70 percent of sales revenue and 74 percent of profit and tax remittances.[69] This finding is consistent with the new guiding theme, "seize the big and release the small" (*zhuada fangxiao*), promulgated by state leaders.[70] In the words of Jiang Lemin of the Ministry of Finance, "We no longer need to run tens of thousands of state firms. It is enough to control the key companies that direct the national economy. A large portion of the small and medium-sized firms will leave the state sector, and the workers will no longer be the state's responsibility."[71]

For the three above-mentioned reasons, it seems likely that SOEs will continue to play a prominent role in the foreseeable future, and that commercial considerations will not be the only factors guiding the decisionmaking process of state leaders and SOE managers. To have SOEs operate according to commercial considerations would mean that some 30 million people will become unemployed overnight—a fact not lost on the state leadership in Beijing. Consequently, it seems likely that SOEs will play a prominent role in the reform economy.

While SOEs make up a steadily smaller percentage of gross-value industrial output—roughly some 28 percent in 1998—it is wrong to discount the important role that SOEs continue to play. State-owned enterprises still employ roughly two-thirds of urban industrial workers, and state leaders routinely proclaim that "state-owned enterprises, particularly large and medium-sized ones, are the mainstay of the national economy."[72] President Jiang Zemin himself continues to remark that China is a socialist-market economy—which it cannot be "if public ownership is not made the main component."[73] Furthermore, as Jiang continues,

> Expanding the state-owned economy is the basic guarantee for building socialism with Chinese characteristics. As always, the public sector occupied a dominant position in important and key trades and spheres of the national economy, controlled the economic lifelines of the country, and had supremacy and predominance over other economic sectors.[74]

Statism and Industrial Policy. Currently, the WTO does not oversee and has no mandate to rule on broad issues of corporate governance structure or industrial policy, whereby the Chinese government provides preferential policies to firms to turn them into "national champions." Not surprisingly, China's trading partners take exception to this intervention, regardless of the bailout, infant-industry, or national-champion justification.[75] U.S. trade officials routinely express their displeasure with the pillar- or infant-industry-promotion strategy of the Chinese government, which "indicates the strong hand of industrial policy in actually skewing the market."[76]

China has done little to demonstrate that it is backing away from heavy-handed industrial policies. In the case of pillar industries, for example—industries targeted for state promotion through such policies as tax credits and low-interest loans from the state-banking system—one state official described the strategy as follows: "The state needs to build up a number of key industrial projects, of a high standard and on a large scale. . . . To develop the pillar industries, we must follow the law of large-scale modernized production and insist on organizing our construction in accordance with the demand of economies of scale."[77] In addition, the Chinese government has long held a policy of directing foreign investment into particular industries.

There is little evidence that this policy is changing, with one article in the state-run *China Daily* recently noting that "China should reshuffle policies on using foreign capital with priority given to the high-tech field and industries with greater market prospects."[78]

It is notable that such actions are consistent with what many observers conclude is a pervasive statist theme common to all the economic reforms in China. These actions should give considerable pause to those arguing that China is moving on a linear path toward a Western-style market economy. As Dorothy Solinger argues with regard to the economic reforms in the PRC at large, "statism is behind the reform effort" where reform is "merely a means, a set of tools to be manipulated in the service of a few fundamental and overarching statist ends: the modernization, invigoration, and enhanced efficiency of the national economy and its consequently heightened capacity to boost both productivity and returns to the central state treasury."[79]

It seems reasonable to conclude, then, that the state will continue to play a prominent role in the economy for years, if not decades, to come. Even in issues as basic as prices, the state still maintains that it will continue to intervene. In the autumn of 1998, for example, the State Economic and Trade Commission proclaimed that market-driven prices in some sectors were too low, resulting in increased losses for state-owned enterprises and a decline of state revenues. Consequently, it issued regulations on twenty-one major goods, including glass, concrete, cars, and sugar. In their defense, state officials remarked:

> The Price Law clearly defines that the price system of this market economy is a market-driven price system under the State's macro control. . . . The law stipulates that to stabilize the general level of market prices is an important goal of the State's macro control and the government should take a series of economic, legal and administrative measures to balance the overall market price . . . to protect consumers' price interests.[80]

The Chinese government's ambivalence toward commitment to a market economy reinforces the main theme of this study: major administrative and judicial reforms must be in place in order to resolve commercial disputes within China and disputes regarding China's obligations as a member of the WTO.

Specific Negotiating Issues

Aside from these broader questions and the central theme of this book—transparent institution building—the working party on accession is addressing a number of specific issues as well. The following section will address some of the major sectoral issues on the negotiating table. A cautionary note for the reader is in order: some of the offers made by the Chinese are informal ones, reflecting the public statements made by Chinese government officials rather than the text of the accession Protocol itself. For example, after Premier Zhu's visit to the United States in April 1999, the USTR office publicized the concessions and commitments on market access made by the Chinese. Although the United States considered these to be commitments, China took a markedly different view and soon began backing away from some the concessions it made. In May 1999 the vice minister of foreign trade and head of China's negotiating team, Long Yongtu, remarked that the USTR list was "not a fair statement because they never showed the paper to us before they announced it. Many of the things in their paper are just not things we have agreed [to implement]."[81] As such, it is possible and perhaps likely that an economic downturn (or even upturn) could dramatically alter the official offer made by the Chinese. Still, although the degree of liberalization and even the general topics are subject to change, the discussion below does highlight those sectors that will likely be difficult.

Industrial Tariffs (Nonagricultural). The most considerable progress made by the PRC in liberalizing its trade regime has been on the tariff front. In April 1996 the PRC lowered the general level of tariff rates on imports from 36 percent to 23 percent. In October 1998 it slashed its average tariff rate from 23 percent to 17 percent on some 5,000 commodities, or 73 percent of all tariff-imposed commodities. In numerous speeches and policy statements, the PRC has announced its intention of achieving an average tariff rate of 15 percent by the year 2000. In light of the market-access package advanced during Zhu Rongji's April 1999 visit to the United States, China agreed (according to a USTR press release) to reduce its tariffs even further—to an average level of 9.44 percent. Two-thirds of these tariff cuts will be implemented by 2003, with the balance to be phased in by 2005, except for a very small number of products. According to the USTR press release, China also "will accept a legal commitment not to raise tariffs in the future above the bound level"—something that very few countries have done.[82]

The United States believes it has secured an even better deal for what it considers to be priority products, where the average tariff will fall to 7.1 percent. Of particular interest to U.S. firms is China's agreement to implement the Information Technology Agreement (ITA), which will reduce tariffs from the present level of 13.3 percent to 0 percent for semiconductors, computers, computer equipment, telecommunications equipment, and other information technology–related products. Other high-priority sectors where China made significant reforms in the April market-access package include forestry products, environmental goods and services, energy and energy equipment, chemicals, toys, gems, and medical equipment.[83]

Undoubtedly, much of the impetus for this lowering of tariff levels has been the Chinese leadership's perception of their own self-interest. In addition to lowering the costs of imported inputs and goods, high tariffs have fostered the growth of smuggling, as the PRC government acknowledges. And notably, China has actually received much less from the imposition of tariffs than the tariff rates might lead one to believe. As the World Bank observes, "A distinctive feature of China's tariff regime is its relatively minor contribution to revenue generation. . . . In large part, it is China's extensive import duty exemptions and rebate system that account for such low collection rates."[84] Moreover, as the PRC government itself notes, the policy of collecting import duties at the border "was inconsistently enforced [and] difficult to regulate." Consequently, "the actual level of tariffs China collected was far below the nominal tariff rates."[85]

Agriculture. Broadly speaking, the debates over accession in agriculture fall into three categories: (1) tariff levels; (2) tariff-rate quotas; and (3) sanitary and phytosanitary standards. Progress on all three was considered very slow until the visit by Zhu Rongji to Washington in April 1999. The slow pace of reform in this sector in the past stemmed from two fears of the Chinese leadership. As Yang explains, "China's desire for agricultural protection stems from its food self-sufficiency policy—a remnant of the Cold War era, when China was afraid of a Western blockade of food supplies. More recently, as the income gap between rural and urban populations widens, trade policy has been advocated to achieve greater income equality."[86] Indeed, despite the significant liberalizing reforms that have taken place in agriculture, a strong element of statism is still pervasive, undoubtedly reflecting the Beijing leadership's goal of state-building. In elaborating on the "mixed nature of the reforms" in agriculture, Thomas Bernstein notes that the actions of the state leadership "were attempts to combine socialist features and predominance with nonsocialist features. . . . The leaders allowed peasant families to contract for land, but they didn't allow them to own the land. They allowed private enterprise to do business, provided it didn't threat the socialist essence in doing so."[87]

The visit by Zhu Rongji, however, appears to have resolved many of these issues surrounding agriculture. According to the USTR press release, China "will reduce tariffs immediately on accession, and when fully phased in will [have] tariff levels comparable with or better than those of many of our other major trading partners (including developed country trading partners)."[88] Moreover, similar to manufactured goods, all agricultural tariffs will be bound and not subject to increase. China will also agree to reduce its average tariff for agricultural products to 17 percent. More significant reductions in tariffs for key commodities will take place by 2004. For example, the present tariff on beef products is 45 percent, but will be reduced to 12 percent by 2004; similarly, the present tariff on citrus products and dairy products hovers in the 30–40 percent range, but will be lowered to roughly 12 percent by 2004.[89]

The second area in agriculture where progress has been made is the tariff-rate quota (TRQ) system, which allows a certain quota of goods to enter at a low tariff rate, but then imposes a higher rate to those goods that exceed the threshold. China has agreed to eliminate this form of quantitative restriction except in some particularly sensitive sectors, such as wool and palm oil, which are not considered priority sectors for the United States. Significant progress has been made in soybean oil, wheat, corn, rice, cotton, and barley. Perhaps more important, though, is that the USTR appears to have secured a deal that would "maximize the likelihood that the full quota would be used and ensure opportunity for private traders to participate, both by allocating an initial share of the quota to private traders and providing for reallocation of quota from state enterprises to private traders if state enterprises do not buy the full TRQ amount."[90]

The third area of disagreement in the agricultural realm involves trade barriers to protect domestic producers from pests or diseases. WTO rules stipulate that such barriers are legal but must be based on "sound science." China, for example, had long restricted U.S. citrus imports because of the fear of medfly infestation. And since the late 1970s, China had refused to import wheat grown in the Pacific Northwest region of the United States because such wheat contains the fungus *tilletia controversa kuhn*, also known as TCK smut. While the United States claimed that TCK smut is a minor disease, China in the past agreed only to send scientists over to study it. And even this concession was made only after Senator Max Baucus (D-Montana), widely viewed as a moderate on China, complained that his "patience is wearing very thin" on China's lack of progress on market access.[91]

Significant progress on the sanitary and phytosanitary issue was made in April 1999 with the signature of three bilateral agreements, concluded in tandem with the other market-access issues concerning China's WTO accession. With regard to meat products, China agreed to accept USDA certification for U.S. exports. In citrus, China agreed to implement a science-based phytosanitary system and to eliminate a ban on products such as oranges and grapefruit. Citrus industry officials estimated that as a result of this breakthrough, citrus exports to China would increase by some $700 million, to a total of $1.2 billion. Another major breakthrough occurred in wheat products, with China agreeing to eliminate restrictions on wheat imports from the Pacific Northwest because of TCK smut.[92]

Telecommunications. The degree of market access granted to foreigners depends greatly on the specific type of telecommunications service being offered. Overall, though, the sector remains quite restricted. While serving as premier, Li Peng commented that "China would like to carry out extensive cooperation with foreign telecommunications companies in technology," but that this must be "mutually beneficial cooperation focusing on technological exchanges with Chinese companies."[93] In practice, this has meant that foreign involvement in the telecommunications sector is still quite limited. Prior to the April 1999 visit by Zhu Rongji, there appeared to be regression in this area. An unpublished report from the Chinese State Council (the equivalent of the U.S. cabinet) criticized foreign joint ventures and wholly owned subsidiaries for resisting the transfer of technology to Chinese equipment makers. The Chinese leadership even drew up a plan to reduce the market share of foreign telecommunications-equipment makers over the next five years, replacing that share with the

Chinese infant industry, to be developed by governmental support for local firms.[94]

After Zhu's visit, the USTR reported that China agreed to become a member of the Basic Telecommunications Agreement and would implement the required procompetitive regulatory principles. China also agreed to phase out geographic restrictions over four to six years, depending on the specific type of service. Moreover, China would allow 49 percent-foreign ownership in all services.

The problem with this agreement is that the minister of information industries, Wu Jichuan, attempted (apparently unsuccessfully) to resign after Zhu returned from Washington because he had not agreed to Zhu's promises. That Minister Wu took this position is not surprising. When asked why past offers on telecoms have been so limited, PRC officials often quote the well-known Chinese saying, "Things will be settled once conditions are ripe" (*guashu dailuo*). According to the PRC leadership, the situation in many parts of the telecom industry is far from ripe. In the words of Minister Wu, "We still have difficulties in letting foreign counterparts get involved in China's telecom-service sector, because the conditions are not ripe."[95]

One sticking point remains the provision of basic telecommunications services in the rural areas of the PRC. Telephone density is 26.1 percent in urban areas, but it remains only 8.11 percent in the countryside.[96] To bridge this gap and expand services to rural areas, the Chinese government is building a 2,754-kilometer-long optical-fiber line between Lanzhou, the capital of Gansu province, and Lhasa, the capital of Tibet, at an estimated cost of some $80 million. The investment will provide services to consumers previously not provided even with basic telephone service. From the perspective of Minister Wu and the PRC leadership, the problem is that "no foreign investors would have been willing to build this optical link." The PRC openly acknowledges that long-term state policy can override profit motives, but as Minister Wu continues, "Foreigners, when they come, are after profit. As minister, I would not like to share policy-based profits with them."[97] For this reason, Wu has decided that foreign investment can be used for financing equipment but that foreigners are not allowed to operate networks. This situation will likely remain in effect until 2010.

Not surprisingly, foreign companies have taken a dim view of this position, with some forty-six joining together to send a letter in confidence to Prime Minister Zhu Rongji asking him to intervene personally to allow greater access and "normal equity participation" (the contents of the letter were subsequently leaked).[98] Interestingly, though, some of the greatest pressure for change has come from within the PRC itself. It is now common to read in a newspaper or hear on radio reports that "the monopoly on telecommunications is harmful to consumers and the telecommunications industry itself. This industry represents only 5 percent of the national economy, but influences the development of the remaining 95 percent." One also reads that "the ministry, in being the regulator and operator of the network, develops all sorts of policies and rules for maintaining its monopoly position, seriously ignoring the interests of the country and the people."[99]

Some progress has been made in breaking up China Telecom. Dissatisfied with the monopoly, a number of interest groups, including competing ministries, effectively pressured the leadership to allow the creation of a second carrier, China Unicom. (China Telecom's revenue base is still some 112 times the size of China Unicom's, however.)[100] China Unicom is currently the one vehicle through which foreigners can invest in basic telecommunications services in the PRC, although the method is circuitous. Foreign companies cannot invest directly in China Telecom operators; instead, they must fund a Chinese company, in this case China Unicom, to invest in another Chinese company. There have been some twenty-three joint-venture contracts of this kind, worth some $U.S. 1.5 billion.

Despite the creation of this second carrier, the pricing of many of the services offered—even by China Unicom—is still controlled by the state. More important, the Chinese government has recently agreed to split China Telecom into smaller, regional-based companies that will provide local phone service, cell-phone operations, satellite transmissions, and paging. Although China Telecom will maintain its international service franchise and this breakup will not directly affect foreign companies, it should pave the way for resolving the foreign-investment issue.

Market access to other telecommunications services, however, is likely to be more open in the future, because there is already significant domestic competition within the PRC. China is the largest single market in the world for telephone-paging services, for example, boasting some 50 million subscribers. Although China Telecom holds a roughly 75 percent market share, that share has been eroding, as there are now thousands of competitors in the paging market. Similarly, in the mobile-phone industry, it is estimated that the number of subscribers will rise to some 30 million users by the year 2000;[101] currently there are estimated to be between 12.5 and 14 million mobile-phone users. Mobile handsets built by foreign companies almost completely dominate the market, with Ericsson, Motorola, Nokia, and Siemens controlling roughly 92 percent of market share. Motorola, which began investing in the PRC in 1986, was the first U.S. company to be allowed 100 percent ownership of its operations in the mainland; it has now established seven joint ventures as well.[102] Domestic competition also exists in Internet-service providers. Currently, about 100 providers exist for some 400,000 official users in China. It is estimated that the number of users might be four times this amount, considering that individuals often share accounts.[103]

Other Services. Service sectors, which are commanding increasing importance in trade and investment flows, together constitute far and away the largest area of disagreement among the PRC, the working party, and individual nations such as the United States. Although the PRC has begun to soften its hard-line stance in this area, the bulk of the negotiating decisions have yet to be made. The perception of the Chinese leadership is revealed in the words of one negotiator: "If we have to open up our relatively backward service market overnight, it will quickly be destroyed and have nothing to gain in the long term."[104]

Some of these fears on the part of the Chinese are legitimate. In the area of financial services, in particular, the banking system could collapse if not handled properly. Currently the state-run banking system, which is crucial to channeling investment to state-owned enterprises, is held afloat by personal deposits that account for some 70 percent of all assets. Since the average saving rate in China is 40 percent, there is a great deal of discretionary income that could be shifted to alternative sources if financial-service liberalization occurs.[105] For this reason, as Barry Naughton explains, "Greater capital account liberalization might lead to financial crisis if Chinese citizens are given the option to transfer funds on a large scale from the domestic banking system to other—particularly international—assets."[106]

In light of this concern, we should view the progress made during the April 1999 visit as significant. Specifically, the proposed agreement would allow 100 percent-foreign investment in retail banking by 2005. Two years after China's entry into the WTO, foreign banks would be allowed to handle local-currency business for Chinese companies, and they would be able to provide foreign-exchange services to individuals after five years.[107]

The specifics of the details are not yet worked out, as China insisted that it would remove financial-services concessions if the United States did not back down on textiles. Still, the events of April suggest considerable progress over past developments in financial services. For example, by the end of 1997 China had approved the founding of only 162 foreign-funded financial institutions engaged in business operations (excluding insurance). These institutions comprised 142 foreign-branch banks, 5 exclusively foreign-funded banks, 7 Sino-foreign jointly funded banks, 1 Sino-foreign investment bank, and 7 exclusively foreign-funded and Sino-foreign jointly funded financial companies. By the end of 1997 China also had 363 representative offices of foreign-funded financial institutions (excluding insurance), including 277 banks, 58 securities companies, 9 credit card companies, 6 financial companies, and 13 other businesses. Only twenty-four cities were allowed to set up foreign-funded financial businesses on a trial basis.[108]

The figures cited above exclude the insurance sector, where progress has been quite slow. Again, the Chinese government invokes an infant-industry argument. As reported in one article in *Beijing Review* in November 1998, "Because China's commercial insurance sector developed relatively recently, the insurance system is still incomplete. Therefore, opening China's insurance market to the outside world should be conducted in a steady and orderly way."[109]

Specifically, foreign insurance companies may operate only in Shanghai and Guangzhou. By the end of 1997, the two pilot cities had approved nine foreign-funded insurance businesses, including eight branches of foreign insurance companies and one Sino-foreign jointly funded company. Foreign insurance companies have set up 181 representative offices in the country. It is important for them to do this because PRC law stipulates that only insurance companies in operation for more than thirty years, with assets exceeding $U.S. 5 billion, and with representative offices in the PRC for at least two years may set up businesses.[110] Some progress was apparently made during Zhu's visit, with the USTR reporting that China will eliminate some geographic and numerical limitations, depending on the type of insurance being provided. Specifically, China will open up twenty-four cities to U.S. insurance companies. Apparently China will also allow 51 percent-ownership in joint-ventures, something it has adamantly refused to do in other sectors, such as telecommunciations.

Intellectual Property Rights. It might seem that intellectual-property-rights (IPR) protection should not be a major issue of contention in the accession of China to the World Trade Organization.[111] China has already agreed to abide by most international treaties on IPR, including those that originated in GATT. The launching of the WTO in 1995 coincided with the commencement of the GATT Uruguay Round Agreement on Trade Related Aspects of Intellectual Property Rights (TRIPs). This agreement reflected growing concern over intellectual-property-right infringement in certain countries. The PRC has agreed to abide by TRIPs once it becomes a WTO member, and it has already taken steps to comply with the agreement.[112] While there are undoubtedly areas where China's intellectual-property laws are substandard, recent judicial and administrative decisions in China indicate a clear trend toward greater protection of IPR.

Surely the U.S. government welcomes the signing of the TRIPs agreement by China, but it is clear that the IPR issue significantly clouds the two nations' bilateral trading relationship. The United States is demanding greater assurance that infringement of IPR will be dealt with fairly and expeditiously. Part of the confusion stems from the complexity of the legal institutions in the PRC designed to address IPR infringement. A key distinction between IPR enforcement in the PRC and in other countries is that one has the option of administrative or judicial recourse in dealing with infringement. China's courts share adjudicative power with other quasi-judicial bodies, such as administrative agencies and other commissions vested with collective authority to settle disputes. In essence, the courts are equal counterparts to the bureaucratic agencies of the Chinese state. Technically, one can pursue both administrative action and court action. In practice, however, the judicial system often denies intellectual-property-rights holders' requests for administrative action if a lawsuit is pending in the People's Court.[113]

With regard to administrative agencies, the PRC has established a number of governmental institutions—arguably too many. The primary governing bodies include the State Press and Publication Administration, the National Copyright Association, the China Patent Office, and the State Administration of Industry and Commerce, in which the Trademark Office is located. The PRC also recently announced the formation of the Ministry of Information Industry. And in the spring of 1998 the state announced the creation of the State Intellectual Property Office (SIPO) at the subministerial level, attached directly to the State Council. As one state official notes, "The new office will take on greater responsibility for improving China's trademark, copyright, and patent application and management, and other aspects of intellectual property rights."[114]

With regard to judicial proceedings, one positive development has been the establishment of specialized intellectual-property courts. This development is relatively recent. In July 1993, China established a specific intellectual-property chamber in the Beijing Higher People's Court and Intermediate People's Court. As of 1998, twenty such IPR tribunals had been established in Higher and Intermediate People's Courts.[115]

There are several problems, however, with having so many different agencies and venues in which to redress IPR infringement. One problem, as described by a PRC official, "is related to the fact that there are so many laws, the limits of authority intersect, and the ability to handle cases and sense of duty are not strong enough for the present situation."[116] The other problem concerns what the Chinese refer to as "too many mothers-in-law" (*po po tai duo*, or *yi ge shifu, san ge po po*); the practical effect is that different ministries are pitted against one another. The State Drugs Bureau, a functional subsidiary of the Ministry of Public Health, allows pharmaceutical companies to use registered trademarks of competing products as it promotes public health. Not surprisingly, those in favor of trademark protection take a dim view of this activity. The result is that "the relocation of administrative powers has caused problems in enforcement of legal rights, as orders may come from different administrations having cross-jurisdiction on a matter. In the 1999 *Weitai* case, the plaintiff pharmaceutical company was the registrant of a mark for a popular stomach drug. The defendant used the mark on its competing product. As such, the case placed the State Administration for Industry and Commerce in opposition to the Ministry of Public Health.[117]

This problem is not lost on the top leadership. Indeed, as one Chinese official notes, "Many enterprises have made it known that there should be a chief enforcement agency that combines both the power and the responsibility in one place for the task of IPR protection . . . [so] that the shifting of responsibilities onto others is avoided."[118] Arguably, this is the reason why the State Council created the State

Intellectual Property Office in the spring of 1998. Although this appears to be a step in the right direction, SIPO is not the sole agency in charge of IPR enforcement. SIPO will primarily handle patent issues and take on greater responsibility for trademarks and copyrights. As for the State Administration of Industry and Commerce and the State Press and Publication Administration, "The new SIPO will work with these two departments, to improve intellectual-property-rights protection nationwide."[119] It remains to be seen how effective this cooperation will be in curtailing and preventing future IPR infringement.

Concluding Remarks on Sectoral Negotiations

Although these sector-by-sector negotiations are important to key manufacturing and service-sector interest groups, and agreements seem close on most of the major issues, even more important is the establishment of an institutional framework that will not only help China along the path of reform but will afford WTO members an objective means to evaluate its reforms. The historical record makes it clear that particular timetables often become irrelevant in light of major shifts in economic events. Consider, hypothetically, the case had China actually joined the WTO in 1996 or 1997. Undoubtedly the economic and financial crisis afflicting Asia would have led to quite different actions on the part of WTO members. The U.S. demurral from initiating antidumping investigations of several Asian countries after the revelation of the severity of the economic crisis attests to this geopolitical reality.

Broadly speaking, we concur with President Clinton's remark to the Chinese: "China is an emerging economy, so you should have longer phase-ins."[120] It is most important to keep China on the path of reform and to transform its perception of its own self-interest. We believe that an international institution such as the WTO can help bolster China's reform leadership against powerful hard-liners. International institutions can tie the hands of leaders in ways that the ineffectual bilateral relationship is not able to do. WTO is by no means a panacea to China's economic problems, but both China and the world trading community will be better served if China is a member. In the following chapters, we place this idea in historical context and develop specific recommendations for accelerating China's accession to the WTO.

3

————————— 虎 —————————

Nonmarket Economies and the WTO

To understand the difficulties attendant on full Chinese membership in the WTO, we should review and consider the history of nonmarket economies (NMEs) in the world trading system since World War II.

A Historical Perspective

The post-World War II trading system was not built on pure free-trade theory. The leaders of the effort to establish an International Trade Organization (later the GATT) believed that unilateral disarmament in trade, although implicitly called for in the writings of Adam Smith, was not politically viable because of the strong power of domestic-producer interests in each country. These leaders did introduce one major advance for more universal liberalization—the principle of unconditional most-favored-nation (MFN) status, according to which concessions granted to one country in the GATT must be extended to all other members. Along with MFN, however, they also created the highly successful, if economically flawed, system of reciprocal negotiations, according to which it was assumed that benefits and concessions would be more or less balanced at the end of the day. This was in reality a kind of benign mercantilism, in which nations demanded "reciprocal" concessions from other nations for taking steps (such as opening markets) that would benefit their own economies in any case.

The GATT also deviated from pure market theory by not attempting to outlaw or condemn state monopolies. At the time of its founding and for many years thereafter, many "market economies" retained public control over purported strategic sectors. As John Jackson has pointed out, a number of GATT members "desired to ensure the state's right to actively manipulate market variables."[1] GATT Article XVII, which deals with state enterprises, lacks real teeth and reflects the ambivalence of member-states on these issues. It is largely hortatory, declaring merely that state trading enterprises should "act in a manner consistent with general principles of nondiscriminatory treatment described in this agreement."[2]

Article XVII does prescribe that in any purchase of goods, the state enterprise must act "in accordance with commercial considerations, including price, quality, availability, marketability, transportation, and other conditions of purchase or sale."[3] Yet a number of problems and loopholes remain, as commentators have observed. These include the determination of the meaning of the phrase *according to commercial considerations*; verification of compliance with WTO rules in economies where quotas and production mandates, not tariffs, are the primary methods of import control; and resolution of problems when the state trading company does not in fact exercise an import monopoly.[4]

Although the GATT from the outset included members with socialist regimes and large-scale government ownership and control over major sectors, its rules did not anticipate the prospect of many members whose entire economies were based on state trading principles. Indeed, even after fifty years of GATT and WTO law, there is still no widely accepted set of criteria for distinguishing a market from a nonmarket economy. In the past, GATT members with command-and-control economies were few in number and small in size, so this issue was manageable. Now, with the imminent arrival on the WTO doorstep of seventeen former Communist, state-controlled economies, a major challenge looms for fundamental WTO principles and rules.

The fact that every new candidate for WTO membership is engaged in an economic transition toward market-based principles increasingly complicates the issue. For the purposes of this volume it is important to establish certain guideposts regarding the Chinese economy that demonstrate evidence of the transition away from a purely nonmarket economy. As was noted earlier in this book, import- and export-licensing arrangements were introduced in the early 1980s—

actually as a liberalizing measure—to replace an existing trade monopoly. In the 1990s, even licensing provisions were drastically curtailed.

Market pricing, however, constitutes the most important signal that an economy is moving away from command-and-control, statist policies. Here, the primary Chinese transitional device was the creation of a two-tiered pricing system under which the command price operated for a fixed quantity of a commodity, but producers were allowed to supply additional output at a secondary, market-determined price. Gradually, this transitional pricing system has been abandoned. In 1995 more than 90 percent of retail commodities were market-based, as were more than 80 percent of agricultural products and capital goods.

Despite these changes in the Chinese economy, the accession process is complicated by the fact that decades ago some unfortunate precedents were established specifically regarding some very small East European economies—Yugoslavia, Poland, Hungary, and Romania—for dealing with NMEs in general. Below, we discuss the cases of Poland and Romania.

The Case of Poland. In 1967, Poland became the first nonmarket economy to achieve membership in the GATT, and its terms of accession, along with alternate schemes devised for Hungary and Romania, have been cited as potential guides for China, Russia, and former Soviet states. In devising a suitable "entrance fee" for the Polish accession, GATT members deemed that the traditional fee of equivalent tariff reductions to "pay" for the tariff concession previously negotiated in the GATT was not appropriate, in that tariff levels in nonmarket economies were meaningless as regulators of future imports. (Under the planned economies, imports and exports were determined administratively as part of a detailed national plan.)

A number of proposals were put forward, but in the end Poland agreed to a managed-trade solution in which it undertook to increase the total value of its imports from market economies by not less than 7 percent per annum. In addition, GATT members were allowed to use selective safeguards in cases where import surges from Poland "caused or threatened to cause serious injury to domestic producers of the same or directly competitive products."[5] This clause departed significantly from the existing safeguard provision of Article XIX of the GATT, which applied restrictions to all GATT members and did not allow the exemption of one nation. Furthermore, at the insistence of the European Union (EU), discriminatory quantitative restrictions were allowed, with no date set for their elimination. This provision produced a pitched battle between the EU and the United States, with the U.S. State Department labeling the EU the "incarnation of international commercial evil."[6]

In the current debate over China's terms of accession, both import targets and selective safeguards have been advocated as solutions to the problem of asymmetric import access. Putting aside the safeguard issue for the moment, the history of the "7 percent solution" is instructive and damning. It contains both ideological and practical problems. First, the formulaic, fixed-import commitment contradicted the market-oriented philosophy behind the GATT and invited government intervention with administrative measures to control imports. Second, the commitment left open the possibility of discrimination among exporting countries. On the practical side, it was based on current prices, and thus it eroded as inflation occurred later. Furthermore, the commitment was denominated in Polish currency, and it invited manipulation of the exchange rate. Finally, there was a built-in disincentive to allow import growth beyond 7 percent, in that overfulfillment of one year's target would increase the base for the next year, making subsequent targets ever more difficult to meet.

The actual history of Poland's trade numbers bears out the fears of the time regarding the creation of disincentives to trade. In the years following 1968 Poland exceeded the 7 percent agreement, but this changed in 1977, when Poland failed to meet the target.[7] The consequence of the managed-trade solution, however, was clear: "The Polish formula . . . turned out to have been ambitious in requiring a 7 percent annual increase in imports. Poland's inability to meet that figure caused it to elect to reduce its export levels. The rigid quid pro quo resulted in the reduction of Poland's trade with GATT signatories from levels otherwise possible."[8]

The Case of Romania. With the Polish experience fresh before it, Romania adamantly and successfully opposed a specific import commitment; rather, its protocol merely stated that Romania "firmly intends to increase its imports from the contracting parties as a whole at a rate not smaller than the growth of total Romanian imports provided for in its five-year plans."[9] Romania was forced, however, to accept discriminatory safeguards as well as quantitative restrictions (QR) still demanded by the EU. Of relevance to the Chinese situation, it should be noted that the EU as a whole did not apply the QRs—rather, individual EU nations applied them. This specificity produced a tremendously complex set of trade rules between Romania and the other nations of Europe—a situation that would surely be multiplied manifold with a trading nation as large and important as China. Looking back even on the less stringent terms forced upon Romania (and later Hungary), one commentator concludes,

> [These commitments] are also vague to the point of being unenforceable. Moreover, such commitments share a basic conceptual weakness with the whole notion of import commitments: they are at best a surrogate for the liberalization of trade mechanisms. . . . Import commitments not only leave the goal of trade liberalization unachieved, but possibly reinforce trade distortions.[10]

The analysis and recommendations in the following sections are based on the reality that China—and all the former Communist states applying for WTO membership—are neither completely market nor completely nonmarket economies. Given this circumstance, the overarching goal of accession rules regarding trade remedies should be to create incentives throughout the process that will impel firms and government agencies in these countries to adopt market options and policies.

Contingency Protection and Chinese Accession

In the April negotiations, U.S. and Chinese negotiators remained completely at odds over contingency protection measures—safeguards against import surges and antidumping rules. The Chinese strongly resisted a separate regime tailored specifically to their economy, while U.S. trade officials held out for open-ended authority to protect U.S. industries from what they termed "unfair competition" and "import surges." Subsequently, U.S. Commerce Department Secretary William Daley repeatedly promised key U.S. sectors—textiles and steel—that the United States would hold fast on these issues. Although the language of the Protocol will change in details, the main elements of the arguments on both sides are already on the table.[11]

The accession Protocol contains two sections that deal with the issues of safeguards and antidumping laws and regulations. We shall deal with the safeguard issue later in this book. Here, we analyze those issues relating to future antidumping actions that would involve China and other nonmarket economies during a suggested transition period leading to the establishment of full rights in the WTO. This discussion will also necessarily include a consideration of China's bilateral arrangements with key WTO members, such as the EU and the United States, on antidumping.

The issues discussed in this section have implications well beyond China; there are now seventeen transition economies applying for accession to the WTO. Of these, only the Russian and Chinese economies show the potential to exert great influence on world trade in the future. Taken together, however, the other transition economies—the former Soviet republics and the other East European economies—represent a considerable amount of potential trade and investment. The relevant section in the Protocol states:

> It is recognized that, in the case of imports of Chinese origin into a WTO Member, special difficulties may exist in determining price comparability in the context of anti-dumping and countervailing duty investigations. In such cases, the importing country may find it necessary to take into account the possibility that a strict comparison with domestic prices in China may not always be appropriate.[12]

If adopted, the language would in effect allow WTO-member countries to continue to utilize very different systems for handling both dumping and subsidy cases against China, with no termination date or process for integration back into the revised Uruguay Round rules established in these areas. To understand the potential differences, it is necessary to give a brief description of current practices and their effect on trade with China. Under U.S. law, dumping (that is, selling at less than fair market value) occurs when a foreign manufacturer charges a lower price in the United States than in the manufacturer's home market, or a third market, for the same or similar merchandise—and this pricing strategy injures or threatens to injure the U.S. domestic industry.

Since the passage of the 1988 Trade Act, the United States has determined the margin of dumping for so-called nonmarket economies by either of two methods: the "factors of production" method, whereby the NME manufacturer supplies cost data on each input in the manufacture of the article, and the costs of each factor are then calculated from a comparable market economy; and the "surrogate country" method, whereby all data, in cases where input data from NMEs are not available, are drawn from a surrogate country of comparable economic development. In the EU, costs and prices are simply obtained from a third country.[13]

The evolution of U.S. laws and regulations, more than those of the EU, gives evidence of an acknowledgment of the deficiencies in NME antidumping actions. Unfortunately, even U.S. actions do not go nearly far enough, and in some cases attempted reforms have been thwarted. For instance, initially neither the EU nor the United States published documents defining the differences between market and nonmarket economies. The EU Council of Ministers merely published a list of NMEs in 1982, and then revised and extended it in 1994 to reflect the breakup of the Soviet Union. Although the existence of a market economy with prices that reflect the costs of production is a key determining factor, clearly politics has also played a part for the European Union. Thus, the EU removed Bulgaria and Romania from the list of NMEs, although neither has taken many steps toward the marketization of its economy.

In December 1998, the European Commission tabled a proposal made to the fifteen EU members that would remove the nonmarket-economy designation from the PRC. It is unclear, however, what the practical consequences of that decision will be in the handling of dumping cases. EU antidumping decisionmaking is not transparent to observers, and the commission does not publish the rationale for its rulings. In China's case, the council merely promised to make decisions on dumping allegations on a case-by-case basis.

Market-economy status is also dealt with on a case-by-case basis in the United States, even though the 1988 Trade Act did establish a list of criteria for determining the NME designation. The six factors were: (1) extent to which a nation's currency is convertible; (2) extent to which wages are determined by free bargaining; (3) extent to which joint ventures with foreign firms are permitted; (4) extent of government ownership of means of production; (5) extent of government control over allocation of resources, and over price and output decisions; and (6) other factors that the administering authority considers important.[14]

Several points should be noted about this list. First, the last criterion is open-ended and could permit additional obstacles to be introduced at any point (though in fairness, the Commerce Department, which administers the law, has shown no sign of moving in this direction). Second, there are no quantitative measures; thus, judgment of the evidence of increasing market activity is thoroughly discretionary. This second point was noted by the Commerce Department itself, when it complained in a report to Congress that "because the statute does not assign weights to the various criteria, it is difficult to say which of these factors should be more important in determining whether the country should be treated as a nonmarket-economy country."[15]

The Commerce Department has also acknowledged a more fundamental contradiction in the treatment of NMEs under U.S. antidumping and countervailing duty laws: that is, that the transition economies are in many ways indistinguishable from developing-country market economies *not* governed by special antidumping regulations, and many of these are members of the WTO. One commentator specifically stated: "For example, the governments of developing market-economy countries often heavily regulate foreign exchange and the availability of long-term capital; rely on price controls; and own many of the country's basic industries, much like the economic behavior of the NMEs."[16] Accordingly, in a recent analysis, Seoul University law professor Sanghan Wang concludes:

> Overall, [the criteria] suffer from vagueness and inadequacy. While purporting to address the issue of whether a country is a market economy for fair-value determination purposes, the provision includes criteria which have macroeconomic significance beyond the fair value determination purpose . . . [and] it leaves out an important consideration—whether import decisions are made free or relatively free from government intervention. The vagueness and inadequacy of the criteria suggest the Department of Commerce may grant a market economy status to a country which does not have a market economy, while at the same time refusing to recognize a market economy even if it is one.[17]

Antidumping: The Advance and Retreat of Bubbles of Capitalism

In the early 1990s, the Commerce Department briefly showed signs of flexibility and of an awareness that the prices and markets in rapidly transforming economies created a shifting target. In two antidumping cases related to China (fans and lug nuts exported by the PRC),[18] Commerce wrestled with new methods of calculating prices, costs of production, and ultimately dumping margins by introducing the concept of "bubbles of capitalism." Utilizing new authority under the 1988 Trade Act, Commerce undertook to determine if an individual sector was free enough from state control to justify using its own price-and-production data in calculating any potential dumping margins. The Chinese companies in each case argued that the government had no control over the type or volume of production, price charges, distribution of profits, or the company's right to obtain, use, or dispose of capital. In addition, in the lug nuts case, Commerce further allowed a defendant in an NME to attempt to prove that certain inputs were market-driven and thus eligible for inclusion in later antidumping calculations. (In that case, Commerce found that the prices paid for two key inputs to the manufacture of lug nuts—steel and chemicals—were market-driven.)

These concessions demonstrated that the Commerce Department was at least aware of some of the complexities of the evolving Chinese economy. All too quickly, however—thanks to a combination of technical factors and stinging congressional and interest-group criticism[19]—the department retreated and in effect cut off these pathways to partially market-based analysis. In another case and in a reversal of the original lug nuts decision, the Commerce Department introduced a new concept, the "market-oriented industry approach," which established much more stringent rules for a finding that a manufacturer in an NME was actually a market-economy producer. Reversing its previous open-mindedness, Commerce now expressed deep skepticism that bubbles of capitalism could actually exist in NMEs. The agency stated flatly that in order for it to find that an NME producer was acting as a market-economy producer, it would "have to be persuaded that all prices and costs faced by the individual producer are market-determined."[20]

The Clinton administration made one additional attempt to revise NME antidumping rules and procedures when Congress drafted implementing legislation for the Uruguay Round Agreement. The administration proposed to create a special category of rules for economies in transition, defined in this case as countries instituting the right of private property and establishing a mechanism to privatize state-owned enterprises. Under the new procedures, for a period of five years, the U.S. International Trade Commission (ITC) would assume responsibility for making antidumping decisions for these economies. Substantively, the proposal would have eliminated dumping calculations altogether and mandated relief upon a showing of "serious injury or threat of serious injury"—this was a higher standard than currently existed for relief. Finally, the proposal left to the ITC full discretion to tailor a remedy, and it implicitly encouraged so-called "suspension agreements," in which the NME producer would agree to increase prices or agree to quotas to avoid dumping penalties.[21]

Before discussing the implications of the above-described U.S.-EU treatment of alleged NME dumping for negotiations over Chinese accession into the WTO, a word is in order on the broader implications for world trade and the multilateral trading system. In 1997 the World Bank published detailed analyses of the effects on transition economies of the special antidumping procedures used by the United States and the European Union. The editors of the publication, Constantine Michalopoulos and Alan Winters, pointed out that the studies do not show that the special procedures for NMEs systematically lead to more trade restrictions than do normal antidumping procedures. The editors hasten to add, however, that both the normal and the special antidumping procedures are merely stalking horses for protection: "The main protective effect is a function of the general policies of the EU and the U.S. on antidumping." They also argue that the "most pernicious problem is that . . . the nonmarket economy procedures make it easier to induce price undertaking with exporters and thus to create cartel-like arrangements." They note further (in a point that is of great significance with regard to the current situation in China): "At a time when the transition countries are facing internal difficulties in breaking down existing monopolies and introducing competitive market structure, the last thing they need is externally induced pressures for the introduction of cartel-like arrangements that limit competition and reduce efficiency."[22]

The editors make several recommendations regarding both the antidumping procedures for NMEs and antidumping rules in general. First, they suggest that the United States and the European Union consider whether nonmarket status should be automatically terminated when transition economies achieve membership in the WTO; second, they urge that price undertakings and minimum-price arrangements be abandoned; and finally, in the most far-reaching proposal, they suggest that tests for dumping be made equivalent to domestic tests for predatory pricing, and that user-consumer interests as well as producer interests be factored into dumping decisions.[23]

Lessons for China and the Accession Process

The authors of this volume believe that the aforementioned review of the special NME procedures taken by the European Union and the United States, combined with the analysis and conclusions of the legal experts and economists cited in this volume, contains vital lessons pertaining to Chinese accession into the WTO and the position of the PRC regarding antidumping specifically. First, China is correct in strenuously opposing the open-ended language about dumping currently informing the accession Protocol. This is true for both political and economic reasons. Politically, one reality emerges from the history of attempts by the United States and the European Union to modify the current rigid procedures regarding alleged NME dumping: the power and tenacity of the entrenched interests in both entities to defend the current antidumping system.

An alliance of rent-seeking producers, along with their allies among elected (and, in some cases, administrative) officials and policy analysts dedicated to managed trade, will tenaciously fight to retain the almost-total discretion of the present system. For instance, Greg Mastel of the Economic Strategy Institute had the following reaction to proposals for a new perspective on antidumping:

> This position may make sense from the NME perspective, but it is utterly untenable from the perspective of the United States, and probably that of Europe as well. After all, does the United States really have an obligation to close plants and allow workers to become unemployed so that Russia and China can reduce their unemployment and keep their factories open? Of course not.[24]

Faced with this mind-set, the Chinese are well advised to dig in their heels against the current language of the Protocol. We believe at the same time, however, that the Chinese are making a mistake by thus far adamantly refusing to acknowledge that real problems exist in these areas, and by seeming to adopt a "no-compromise" position. For instance, a former Chinese negotiator stated,"The inclusion of these provisions would . . . nullify China's rights under the WTO. . . . As discrimination in international trade has a special meaning for China, these provisions would certainly not be helpful in engaging China to open its doors to the world."[25] Our recommendations attempt to bridge the gap by accepting that special measures may be necessary during a transition period but must be time-limited and structured to induce market evolution in China.

In a "first-best" world, WTO negotiators would follow the recommendations of Michalopoulos and Winters and, for antidumping purposes, grant automatic market status to transition economies when they become members of the WTO—as well as make dumping tests identical to tests for domestic predatory pricing. Politically, such far-reaching reforms may be impossible; but the PRC is on firm ground in demanding revisions to the rules for dealing with NME dumping procedures as they currently stand in the accession Protocol. First, if special procedures for dealing with dumping are part of the Protocol, China should insist on some kind of sunset clause, or at least a formal process for revising the system when China and other transition economies become true market economies. As an extension of this provision, the Protocol should provide a clear set of criteria for evaluating what constitutes a market economy, along with interim goals for testing China's progress toward meeting those goals. Further, in their individual dumping regimes during any Chinese transition period, the United States and the European Union should establish procedures and regulations for NME dumping cases that foster movement within China toward more market-oriented policies and practices.

While there are many possibilities, we believe that adhering more formally to the bubbles-of-capitalism approach—abortively introduced by the U.S. Commerce Department—would constitute one potentially fruitful reform. Here we agree with the assessment made by Robert H. Lantz, regarding the potential benefits of that or some similar approach. First, it is analytically superior to systems now in use, in that it allows a detailed focus on input costs and introduces a larger degree of predictability in the antidumping process. Second, the bubbles-of-capitalism approach focuses on the individual manufacturer's costs and does not attempt the much more difficult task of determining costs across an entire industry. Lantz foresees substantial market-based benefits from this:

> Using the market-driven costs of an NME manufacturer's domestically-sourced inputs provides an incentive for those

individual manufacturers to continue to operate under market principles. To the extent that the United States export market is important to the success of the NME in transition manufacturers, the manufacturers will reduce their dependence on government subsidies and initiate their own reforms. And third, use of this approach will encourage cooperation in antidumping investigations, because if the NME manufacturer believes that it can persuade the Commerce Department to use its own actual costs in calculating fair market price, it will be more willing to develop and share information.[26]

Safeguards

Tied directly to the issue of antidumping is the demand of some WTO countries that China accept a special transitional safeguard mechanism. Under WTO rules, safeguards are actions that permit temporary protection against "fair trade" caused by a sudden influx of imports that threatens injury to a domestic industry. During the Uruguay Round, rules for safeguards were substantially revised and tightened. Currently, in response to a surge in imports, WTO members may provide relief from competition for a period of four years and then may renew the safeguard provisions under certain restricted circumstances for another four years. The standard for invoking safeguards is that the imports threaten "serious" injury to the domestic industry; this is more stringent than the "material"-injury standard employed for unfair trade remedy cases, such as antidumping actions. In addition, singling out the imports of particular countries (selective safeguards) is not allowed except under extraordinary circumstances—safeguard actions must generally be applied to all imports. Countries invoking safeguard provisions must also take steps to phase out the restrictions over time (degressivity), and to put in place adjustment programs for the industry under competitive pressure.[27]

   The special safeguard provisions suggested in the accession Protocol are much looser and more open-ended. Under these proposals, the PRC would agree to accept, for some unspecified transitional period, both a product-specific safeguard provision and a general safeguard provision. With regard to the product-specific safeguard, the Protocol provides that where imports of a particular Chinese product "have increased in disproportionate percentage in relation to the total increase in imports in the product . . . during the representative period

. . . and are causing or threatening to cause (market disruption) (serious injury: standard yet to be decided),"[28] consultations will be held if there is no agreement, following which the affected WTO member may either withdraw concessions in other areas or limit imports of the specified product. A third WTO member may take similar action, if that member claims that trade is being diverted because of the safeguard arrangement that results from the initial conflict. In each circumstance, China is allowed to take equivalent retaliatory action.

Under the more general safeguard provision, as a result of any "developments in their trade in goods and services" with China, any WTO member can ask for consultations and then, if the member-country cannot agree with the PRC on mutual remedies, that member-country may also suspend concessions or obligations. Once again, the PRC is given the right to suspend its own concessions to an equivalent extent.[29]

The Relation of Safeguards to Antidumping

In the decade before the completion of the Uruguay Round, managed-trade solutions between GATT members flourished, often under the aegis of or as a response to unfair trade laws and regulations. Both the United States and the European Union took the lead in mounting large-scale campaigns to protect key industrial sectors. Sylvia Ostry has explained the changes in the 1980s thusly:

> Perhaps partly as a consequence of the successful tariff reductions in industrialized countries over forty years of multilateral negotiations, these trade remedy measures, especially antidumping, became the trade "weapon of choice" against imports. . . . The trade remedy laws are triggered by industry and administered by the government bureaucracy. They are extremely complex and technical, and their use requires the participation of highly sophisticated (and expensive) lawyers. A built-in momentum has driven the rising frequency of their use, as learning by doing has yielded more procedural expertise on the part of lawyers and more information by business on the opportunities the regulations afford.[30]

Often the real result of antidumping and countervailing duty actions was negotiations that produced informal "voluntary" import or export restraints, usually in the form of quotas. Examples of such arrangements include the United States-Japan and EU-Japan agreements "voluntarily" limiting the importation of automobiles and the United States-Japan semiconductor agreement, which guaranteed (at least according to the United States) foreign importers at least 20 percent of the Japanese semiconductor market.[31]

Legally, all such voluntary agreements were banned in the Uruguay Round agreement. Thus, China's accession negotiations come in the midst of a rethinking by all sides of the use of safeguards as opposed to other trade-remedy laws, particularly in light of the new ban. As noted above, many vociferous U.S. defenders of current antidumping practices give no sign of adapting to the changing legal framework. Mastel, for instance, wrote in early 1998: "In today's international-trade environment, antidumping laws are more essential than ever. . . . There is a compelling historical, legal, moral, and economic case for the continued application of such laws." And on the increased use of safeguard provisions in the place of antidumping or countervailing duties, he observed, "Moving to a system that relied exclusively on safeguard actions would have most of the negative economic impacts of abolishing antidumping laws. Most notably, such a change would have the effect of opening the U.S. economy to nearly unlimited foreign dumping."[32]

Of course, the EU has always taken a more positive attitude about safeguards as a protective device. Indeed it was the EU that demanded quantitative restrictions in the early accession agreements with Poland, Hungary, and Romania—ironically, over vigorous U.S. protests in the name of nondiscrimination. The safeguards that constituted the "entrance fee" to the GATT for the three NMEs also established for the first time a precedent for breaking the cardinal rule of MFN. More recently, in the early 1990s, the association agreements that the EU concluded with the Central European countries contained two highly discretionary general-safeguard provisions, as well as six safeguards specific to particular products or circumstances.[33]

The European Union's affinity for safeguards stems from characteristics of both the EU trading system and the nature of safeguards themselves. The EU has always disliked strong transparency, detailed legal rules, and complex calculations in constructing its trade-remedy system. Thus, its antidumping rules are opaque, and the commission gives little explanation for the basis of its actions.[34] The virtue of safeguards is that they allow even greater discretion and little detailed documentation or protracted legal proceedings. And, unlike Ostry's description of the antidumping system, they do not necessitate a bevy of lawyers or a brace of economists in order to be implemented.

Meanwhile, in the United States there is evidence of some recognition that the challenges by the NMEs to the trade-remedy system may require some melding of antidumping and safeguard rules. The Clinton administration's proposals for changes in the dumping regime for NMEs, as a part of the Uruguay Round–implementing legislation, moved in this direction. The administration proposed that the International Trade Commission eliminate any dumping calculation altogether and provide relief on the basis of a serious-injury standard for the affected industry. (It is interesting to note that the administration also raised the bar by slipping in a serious-injury standard that is tougher to meet than the material-injury standard normally used in antidumping cases. Undoubtedly this was another reason why defenders of dumping laws severely criticized the proposal.) Unfortunately, however, the administration still saw price undertakings as a preferred final result.

Alternative Proposals

This section will explore alternative transitional safeguard systems that could replace what we consider to be the unsatisfactory safeguard proposal currently informing the accession Protocol. We will build on the current negotiations, and on the recommendations advanced by John Jackson and Sylvia Ostry in earlier writings.

In the late 1980s, just as serious accession negotiations for China were getting underway, Jackson suggested elements of an alternative safeguard system designed not only to suit the nonmarket aspects of the Chinese system but also to serve as a precedent for other NMEs, particularly Russia, to follow China into the WTO. He was forthright regarding the three assumptions behind his proposals: first, that "it will be difficult in the long run to deny membership in the GATT to any important nation of the world"; second, that to integrate China, the "GATT has the responsibility to change and to figure out an appropriate way to accommodate different economic systems . . . [while also devising mechanisms] to adequately protect the market-oriented economies from abuse"; and third, that this accommodation would entail the creation of "buffering mechanisms" that "are not very 'pure' in the eyes of market-oriented economic policies."[35] Regarding safeguards specifically, he recommended a "two-track" system. The first track would apply normal WTO procedures to all NME and market-economy members of the WTO. Jackson's proposal predated the Uruguay Round reforms in the safeguards, but those reforms would apply to the first track today.

The second track would be triggered if a WTO government, as the result of a request made by an affected domestic industry, specifically alleged that the imports from an NME were "state trading exports." At this point consultations and a fact-finding process would begin, leading potentially to a finding by the importing country that a serious injury was occurring for the affected industry—and that this was causally related to NME imports. Upon this finding, the importing country would be allowed to apply selective safeguards (import restraints) on these products.

Jackson also suggested limitations and restrictions regarding the second track, including a three-year time limit; some quantitative prerequisites, such as the need to show that state trading imports constituted a certain percentage of all like-product imports; and appropriate adjustment policies for the complaining nation. He also provided for an appeal by the NME to the working party that had handled the accession Protocol.[36]

More recently, in 1993 Sylvia Ostry advanced a similar set of proposals to establish a system of selective safeguards for NMEs under WTO auspices. She argued forcefully that some mechanism of this kind was necessary as a "safety valve," and that "the key is to carefully constrain and discipline the use of the safety valve to prevent its becoming a 'trap door' that permits circumvention of trade discipline all together." Unlike Jackson, Ostry recommended a time limit on the selective-safeguard system she proposed: five years, with the potential for renewal after that time at the discretion of the WTO Council.[37]

For the five-year period, selective safeguards would be allowed against transition economies. A special fast-track WTO panel would be established to grant or reject the safeguard petition from an importing country. Ostry, in contrast to Jackson, suggested that a softer material-injury standard be utilized in place of the serious-injury standard. She suggested no specific duration for the selective restrictions but recommended rather that it be "minimal," and that any extension should invoke significant compensation. Some special transparency mechanism should also be put in place, possibly through the Trade Policy Review Mechanism, to independently monitor the economic effect of the safeguard restrictions on both the NME and the importing-country economies. Finally, and most controversially, she argued that countries invoking the special safeguard mechanism should be required to forgo antidumping and countervailing actions during the time the safeguard restrictions were in place.[38]

Authors' Recommendations

It seems to us that either of these two proposals represents a good starting point for future Chinese-WTO accession safeguard provisions. Picking and choosing among the specific Jackson-Ostry suggestions, we would offer the following. Ostry's idea of a time limitation on the whole process has some merit; there should be some provision for a full-scale WTO Council review of any NME selective-safeguard system, at least within five years. For reasons to be elaborated later in this volume, we also think that the entire process should be integrated into the Trade Policy Review Mechanism (TPRM), with oversight conducted by a special committee of WTO members selected specifically for this purpose.

Regarding the interim special-safeguard system for the PRC, the TPRM committee would be charged with evaluating the facts (such as causality); establishing some minimal criteria regarding quantitative prerequisites, as Jackson suggests; monitoring the process after the safeguard is in place; and overseeing termination or extension of the safeguard action. We agree with recommendations that time limits be placed on the selective safeguard; Jackson's suggestion of three years would be a good starting point for negotiations. Regarding Ostry's suggestion for substantial compensation when an extension is granted, we think this should be handled on a case-by-case basis.

The question of the hard-versus-soft standards depends, in our judgment, on other elements of the proposal. If strict limits are placed on the duration of the safeguard action and if tight quantification standards are also established, then a soft (material-injury) standard might mollify critics of the proposals without doing much harm to the NME exporters. Without such restrictions, however, our predisposition would be to retain the current WTO serious-injury hurdle for the proposed new system.

Finally, we support Ostry's recommendation that WTO members

who opt for selective safeguards against NMEs should be precluded from invoking antidumping and countervailing duty actions during the same period. This will be a hard sell to U.S. trade officials, given the political influence of steel, textile, and semiconductor industries; but we see no need for two bites at the protectionist apple to be taken by local interest groups, abetted by governments.

4

虎

Transparency and Due Process

The central questions of transparency and due process in the Chinese legal system are fiendishly complicated, not only because of the rapid changes taking place in China but also because Chinese accession comes at a time when WTO jurisdiction has widened and deepened. It now encompasses areas far beyond the "border issues" of tariffs and quotas. Furthermore, even the United States, which boasts the most comprehensive administrative law system in the world, is rethinking major elements of its federal administrative procedures and practices.

Why Transparency Matters More Today

Until the Tokyo Round in the late 1970s, GATT negotiations had focused almost exclusively on barriers to trade at national borders. The great achievement of the first GATT rounds was the reduction of average tariffs from higher than 40 percent in 1945 to lower than 10 percent by the early 1980s; by the end of the Uruguay Round, this figure had dropped to 3–4 percent. With the Tokyo Round, GATT rules moved "inside the border"; they began to tackle industrial and agricultural subsidies and antidumping rules. This trend continued with a vengeance in the subsequent Uruguay Round, which dealt largely with so-called new issues—including services, intellectual property, and investment. The Uruguay Round also greatly expanded the rules for agricultural and industrial subsidies and continued to reshape antidumping regulations.

The goal of trade negotiations shifted to a broad concept of *market contestability*. In another publication, we have defined this term and commented on its implications thus:

> A national market is internationally contestable when competition is characterized by rivalry among firms, both domestic and foreign, that is not unduly distorted by anticompetitive government or private action. For the trading system, this will mean that market conditions allow for market access for foreign goods, services, technology, investment and people on terms comparable to those enjoyed by local firms. It will also mean more detailed scrutiny of the actual impact of domestic regulatory, competition and technology policies.[1]

The market-contestability standard drove negotiations deeply into previously domestic questions regarding regulatory reform, defined in both substantive and procedural terms.

The service negotiations in effect concerned competing regulatory systems and "best practices" among them. Indeed, an annex in the service-telecommunications agreement sets forth in detail the substantive rules for competition within the sector. Further, as Sylvia Ostry has noted, the TRIPs agreement "included a detailed enforcement procedure which mirrors step by step the administrative and judicial mechanisms in the United States. . . . A separate council is established to which notification of regulations and administrative arrangements must be made, and this council is mandated to monitor compliance." She concludes, "The shift of trade policy inside the border has created a trading system profoundly different from that designed in the post-war world of shallow integration. And one key feature of that [new] system is a vastly expanded concept of transparency including, as a central feature, the administrative law regimes of WTO member-countries."[2]

Increasingly, attention has been focused on Article X of the GATT, which sets forth rules for the publication and enforcement of trade regulations. With trade-related regulatory systems moving to center stage in trade issues and disputes, Article X is the means by which the first principles of the WTO—most-favored-nation (MFN) status (GATT, Article I), national treatment (GATT, Article III), and nondiscrimination (GATT, Article XIII)—will be realized in the future. Article X requires publication of trade regulations, and it mandates that laws and regulations be administered in a uniform, impartial, and reasonable manner. The contracting parties are also required to establish judicial, arbitrative, or administrative tribunals and procedures to review and correct (if necessary) administrative actions relating to trade. These agencies or courts are to be independent of the agencies initially enforcing national trade regulations—with the additional major loophole that nations may use existing institutions if they provide objective and impartial review, even though they may not be technically independent of the original enforcement agency.[3]

Obstacles in the Chinese Legal and Administrative Systems

Trade and foreign commercial legal issues represent only one facet of the sweeping reforms of the legal system put in motion by the Chinese leaders in Beijing. Both the old system and the emerging new one are multilayered and complex. The Chinese themselves note that crisscrossing jurisdictions, or vertical (*tiao*) bureaucracies and horizontal (*kuai*) coordinating bodies, can lead to organizational and decision-making problems. That is consistent with many other aspects of governmental policymaking in China, resulting in what Kenneth Lieberthal calls "fragmented authoritarianism," with "numerous reporting lines throughout the system—through the party, through the government, to the territorial organs, and so forth."[4] We will describe in this section those characteristics and elements likely to have the most significant effect on WTO-accession rules.

Legislative authority in the PRC is unitary and hierarchical, with the unified power being exercised by the People's Congress and, on a daily basis, by its Standing Committee. In addition, under the People's Congress, the State Council (its executive branch) exercises the power to create ministries and commissions, to pass administrative measures, and, in matters relating to economic reform, to pass actual legislation. The Ministry of Foreign Trade and Economic Cooperation (MOFTEC) is responsible for implementing the Foreign Trade Law, which governs a wide range of trade matters that includes antidumping, the import-export licensing system, foreign joint ventures, customs issues at the border, and the registration of foreign-trade agents.

In theory, local and provincial governments must pass only those laws consistent with the national ones. In practice, although the higher bodies have the authority to disallow conflicting rules, national supervision has little effect on the numerous provincial and local rules created each year. This reality is of great importance to foreign importers and investors, because these local ordinances and regulations form a bedrock of local protectionism.[5]

Commercial disputes in China are handled by two sources: the People's Courts and a variety of arbitration systems. The People's Courts consist of specialized chambers for distinct subject areas, such as civil law, criminal law, foreign business law, and intellectual law. The Supreme People's Court administers the entire system and acts both as a trial court at the national level and as a court of last appeal. Below this stratum are the higher-level and intermediate courts, which also hear trial and appellate cases. Usually, higher-level courts become the venues of first recourse for commercial disputes involving foreign interests.

Under China's Arbitration Law (1994), arbitration committees are being established to handle economic disputes in a number of areas. Arbitration and conciliation involving foreign parties currently fall under the jurisdiction of the China International Economic and Trade Arbitration Commission (CIETAC), which is housed in the China Council for the Promotion of International Trade (CCPIT).[6]

According to foreign observers, although both systems are improving, both continue to suffer from major weaknesses and contradictions. As a legacy of traditional Chinese culture and enduring Maoist influences, for example, courts are still held in low esteem, and the professionalism to be found among lawyers and judges is substandard. Further, in accordance with the 1982 constitution, the courts cannot interfere with the administrative powers of the state. Another problem concerns the fact-finding and decisionmaking processes within courts; they are informal and subject to both outside and inside political influence and second-guessing. Depending on the provincial or local situation, the Communist Party continues to play an important role by staffing with its own members the "adjudication committees" attached to each court; these are empowered to intervene and decide cases. Also, local bosses and interest groups continue to lean on local and provincial courts to change outcomes in their favor. And finally, higher-level courts conduct random reviews of cases handled below them, and where a case is difficult or complex, there is a mechanism for the higher court to render an advisory opinion—a practice that inevitably prejudges any appeal from the original decision.

One commentator has described the role of courts in Chinese society and government thusly:

> In some ways, it would be more accurate to regard [the People's Courts] as but one category among a number of organizations of the state which are required to a greater or lesser extent to interpret and apply laws and regulations. . . . Far from having anything like a monopoly of what in other countries would be regarded as such essentially judicial functions as interpretation of legislation and adjudication of disputes, the courts in China share responsibility for these activities with other "courts"—ministries, commissions and other bodies.[7]

The main reason for this shared responsibility, it is argued, is the "influence of Chinese legal culture, to which Montesquieu's theory of the separation of powers was wholly unknown."

Similarly, the arbitration process, though often fair and effective, also suffers from defects, including ex parte contracts with disputants, political intervention, and a lack of cooperation from other agencies once judgments are rendered. Further, in a recent arbitration, the *Revpower* case, the foreign company found itself unable to enforce the ruling and collect the compensation it was awarded. This failure gave a large black eye to the arbitration process and elicited condemnation from the international arbitration community. (China has signed the New York convention on the Recognition and Enforcement of Foreign Arbitral Awards.)[8]

Conversely, a recent survey of the current operations of the arbitration system for foreign companies concluded that "China has made significant progress over the past decade in developing legal mechanisms for arbitral award enforcement."[9] China has created a dual system, with arbitrations involving foreign companies being handled by CIETAC. The foreign-company process provides greater safeguards against interference by local or provincial courts. Only rarely has it invoked a "social and public interest" clause to deny enforcement, and the process forbids local courts to renege on the enforcement of an award without approval of the People's Supreme Court.[10]

Finally, external to the entire legal and administrative framework are the "normative documents" that constitute one of the most difficult problems for the administration of commercial justice in China. This unpublished body of documents is left over from the pre-reform era when China was governed through administrative decrees and not by legislation, and it is still used extensively by the ministries, commissions, and local enforcement agencies. Although the legal status of the normative documents is today dubious, they remain a potent and binding force in some situations. In the trade arena, MOFTEC vehemently avows its determination to eliminate them. But it is clear that such a reform will be part of an extended and gradual process by which internal procedures and guidelines are to be brought into line with new legislative mandates.

Transparency and the Accession Protocol

What follows is a description of the transparency and administrative-procedure provisions of the accession Protocol, and a brief evaluation of the capability of the Chinese to live up to these obligations under current laws and practices.

Part C, paragraph 1 of the draft Protocol provides that only those laws, regulations, and other measures affecting trade in goods and services that are published and readily available to WTO members, individuals, and organizations shall be enforced. Paragraph 2 requires that China establish or designate a single journal to publish all laws, regulations, and other measures affecting trade.

During the course of the 1993 negotiations, MOFTEC established its own journal to publish all laws, regulations, and administrative rules concerned with foreign trade and investment. It is supposed to contain all laws and regulations published at the national level, but it does not include any relevant provincial or local ordinances. It also does not include normative documents.

Part C, paragraph 1 also requires that China shall make available to outside individuals and organizations all laws and regulations affecting trade before they are implemented or enforced. Though not stated explicitly, the aim of this paragraph seems to be to establish some right of consultation by interested parties before legislation or rules are passed or promulgated.[11]

The quite general mandate asserted in the Protocol leaves many questions unanswered. For instance, is it meant to establish the right of consultation before all draft legislation is passed? Does it include administrative rules and regulations as well? Further, at what stage during the drafting process should consultation take place?

China has never included the right of consultation in either its legislative or its administrative regime. Indeed, only recently did the PRC implement for the highest organs of state—the People's Congress, the Standing Committee, and the State Council—formal rule-making procedures. This new legislative drafting process, however, does include extensive consultations among the relevant ministries, commissions, and party organizations.

There is also a continuing process of drafting a new legislation law, intended to clarify the legislative authority among different organs of state and among different levels of government. The current draft, however, is quite abbreviated and general; it probably reflects infighting among the potentially affected interest groups and state organs.[12]

Administration Litigation and Judicial Review

At the core of the difficulties facing both China and the WTO in fulfilling the obligations for WTO membership are the rudimentary nature of China's administrative law system and the absence of an objective and equitable system of judicial review for administrative decisions. Under the heading Judicial Review, paragraph D of the draft Protocol states:

> China shall establish or designate, and maintain, tribunals, contact points, and procedures for the prompt review of all administrative actions relating to the implementation of laws, regulations, judicial decisions and administrative rulings of general application. . . . The tribunals shall be independent of the agencies entrusted with administrative enforcement.[13]

The perceived weaknesses of Chinese courts have been noted above. Before describing recent changes in the administrative regime, several additional legal and governmental characteristics should be explained. First, the very general nature of Chinese laws and regulations means that it is impossible to determine a legal or practical response without access to the specific administrative rule—or, and here is the flaw-line, access to the relevant normative document. Further, another consequence of the overly broad legislative mandate is the high degree of discretion it gives to Chinese officials in administering commercial laws. They are under no obligation to provide the rationale behind a particular decision.[14]

Two recent legislative enactments, however, may well be harbingers of important changes to come. First is the Administration Litigation Law (ALL) of 1991, which grants to courts the authority to review the lawfulness of certain specific administrative actions, including fines, the restriction of property rights, and the denial of licenses. Excluded from this authority are general administrative acts, such as rulemaking and standard setting. Thus, for national and regional legislation and administrative rules, the People's Courts may ignore regulations promulgated by ministries and provincial governments if there is a legal conflict between those regulations and national laws. Foreigners also have access to the law. In a proceeding, the administrative agency has the obligation to prove, with documentation, that the act or regulation is lawful. Although it looks promising, this act does not represent a major breakthrough because it does not permit review of discretionary decisions, does not review the lawfulness of the underlying regulations upon which a decision is made, and does not apply to Communist Party decisions.[15]

The second positive legislative development is the Administrative Review Regulation (ARR) of 1991, which supplements the changes enacted in the ALL. Specifically, the ARR establishes a system by which administrative acts may be reviewed by a higher-level administrative department. The reviewing department may determine the fairness as well as the lawfulness of a regulation, and the reviewing body has substantially more authority than the courts have to ensure compliance. The disadvantageous aspect of this new allocation of power is the unlikelihood that, under current conditions, higher-level officials will be diligent in overturning a decision taken by bureaucrats in their own department.

Finally, several aborted reform proposals are worthy of note. In the continuous redrafting of the ARR, there has been discussion of a proposal to create a single independent tribunal with broad powers to review the regulations of administrative agencies. This proposal has been rejected, both because it would be inefficient to add another layer of review and because of likely agency opposition. There has also been some discussion about drafting a comprehensive administrative-procedures law, but here, too, agency opposition has proven decisive.[16]

Suggested Revisions in the Draft Accession Protocol

In a recent paper, Robert Herzstein has queried whether, in light of the current weaknesses and contradictions in Chinese law and procedures, the Protocol "should set forth an obligation for China to establish a modern and effective system of administrative law."[17] The implication for the accession process would be that the Protocol would spell out in much greater detail: (1) standards and procedures for businesses to obtain information on government measures that affect a proposed transaction; (2) the means by which business would participate—or at least be consulted—in making laws and regulations affecting business opportunities; and (3) procedures for allowing businesses to contest, before an independent tribunal, government actions they consider improper or illegal.

We the authors agree with Herzstein's suggested proposal, and favor taking his tentative recommendations even further. Our chief additional suggestion is that China be required to establish a separate system of administration and review for disputes relating to trade, investment, and the WTO. Before elaborating on our recommendations, however, we should make two observations: first, a number of administrative regimes could serve as models for China, both in trade and in other areas of law; and second, the administrative rules and procedures of the United States itself have evolved over the past century—and significantly so over the past several decades. Thus, administrative law and procedure are not fixed or immutable. Ultimately, China should be allowed to choose those elements of other national experiences which best fit its needs and social characteristics—as long as it rigorously and definitively administers and enforces whatever system it adopts.

Numerous variations abound of national administrative law systems, but there are two main traditions: the common law tradition of the United States, Britain, and former members of the British Empire, and the civil law tradition of France, Germany, most of Latin America, and many other developing countries. A major distinction between the two systems is the bifurcation of the legal regime into private rights and public rights. In the civil law system, controversies between private citizens over such matters as contracts or liability are handled by ordinary courts. Controversies that pit the citizen (or business organization) against the state, however, are handled by a separate hierarchy of administrative tribunals. In Germany and some other countries, high value is placed on specialized judicial expertise, and many strata of hierarchies deal exclusively with particular types of disputes: tax, social security, or labor relations, for example.[18]

Although modern Chinese legal traditions are still in a rudimentary state, the movement toward a civil law regime may be beneficial for two reasons. First, separate courts would encourage specialization and more sophisticated rulemaking and judicial skill, in both trade and tax law. Second, the operation of private courts would reinforce the emphasis on private rights and obligations. These are different from the public citizenship duties that characterized the former Marxist-Mao "dictatorship of the people."[19]

The difficulty, as usual with China, arises in the blurring of the distinction between public and private obligations and in the encroachment of the public law paradigm—with its emphasis on punitive, and often criminal penalties—on private, commercial law. Though writing specifically about intellectual property rights, Potter and Oksenberg describe the dangers inherent in the entire Chinese legal system thusly:

> Current IPR enforcement reinforces the use of IPR law as an instrument of rule rather than as a mechanism for mediating relations between economic actors. This type of enforcement could result in a system that entrenches the power of the administrative bureaucracy to identify and enforce those rights it considers important, rather than a system that empowers economic actors to identify and enforce their rights to intellectual property. If allowed a greater role, private interests might be more effective in directing IPR enforcement policy toward meeting the interest of economic actors. . . . Foreign governments and corporations should be aware that demands for enforcement are often used by bureaucratic and political interests in China to reinforce statist tendencies or to marginalize private economic actors.[20]

In some countries with civil law systems, such as France and Germany, there has never been a systematic codification of administrative law; it is entirely judge- or court-made. Court-made law might also work to the advantage of the Chinese, over time; if specialization evolves in individual subject areas, then at least pockets of modern legal structure and doctrine will be more likely to expand, whatever the pace of such advances in the Chinese legal system generally. An administrative law system devoted to trade and investment would likely be one of these pockets, for a variety of reasons. For one, both the government and the private sector in China have strong incentives to attract foreign direct investment and trade alliances. Second, after membership is achieved, the government would greatly benefit from the existence of an efficient, advanced trade administration that could lessen the number of private foreign grievances lodged against trade rules and prevent numerous WTO complaints.

There is already precedent in the Chinese legal system for the PRC to create a separate administration to deal with foreign trade and investment matters. Within the People's Court system, for instance, special economic divisions are increasingly tapped to handle litigation involving complex economic judgments, particularly in areas of concentrated commercial activity such as Shanghai, Guangdong, and Beijing.

More formally, in 1993 China began establishing separate courts within the People's Court system to deal with intellectual property cases. By early 1998 there were twenty such Intellectual Property Rights (IPR) tribunals established separately within the intermediate and higher People's Courts system. The situation is complex for several reasons. Claimants still have the right to use the regular People's Courts system, and because these courts can impose harsher sentences, claimants more often use them for more serious alleged infringements. Further, in intellectual property cases, as in other areas of the Chinese legal system, both administrative and legal recourse are available in dealing with infringement. As one commentator has observed, "China's courts share adjudicative power with other semijudicial bodies. Administrative agencies, commissions, and standing state counsels are vested with collective authority to settle disputes."[21]

Further, as has been described above, China has established a separate system of arbitration for foreign enterprises that is presided over by the central trade agency, the China Council for the Promotion of International Trade. We recommend that the Protocol present the outline of a separate system, leaving it to the Chinese to determine the exact details for constructing it. In negotiations, however, the Chinese could be encouraged to build on the model of the IPR court system: that is, to establish within the People's Court system separate specialized courts for foreign-trade and investment disputes. These courts could in the future provide the foundation for creating a cadre of lawyers and judges well versed in WTO rules and procedures. As with the IPR system, it is likely that trade and investment courts would exist alongside both the current system of administrative remedies and the regular People's Court system, to which the claimant would still have recourse should he prefer this route.

Administrative Procedures: How Much Detail?

As we have stated, there are a number of national models for administrative law and regulation from which rules for Chinese WTO accession can be taken. The ultimate solution will need to balance specificity with flexibility, and the goal of objective fairness with the political realities of Chinese politics and legal traditions. In this section we will set forth certain minimum procedural obligations to be followed by whichever authority the Chinese establish or designate to fulfill their WTO-membership requirements.

Before beginning to examine this administrative process, however, we recommend that MOFTEC be designated in the Protocol not only as the "inquiry point" mentioned in the current text but also as the central clearinghouse to which all comments, queries, and complaints can be addressed. As Herzstein and others have pointed out, in the first years after Chinese WTO accession, "foreign companies seeking to do business in China [will certainly] encounter very uneven conditions, lack of transparency . . . perceptions of discrimination or other violations of WTO rules, and inadequate remedies."[22] In addition, it will be important that the governments of other WTO members are able to hold one agency responsible for the handling of subsequent negotiations, inquiries, complaints, and disputes. China should be allowed to change or restructure its trade apparatus in the future, provided that one identifiable organization is given authority commensurate with that exercised by MOFTEC today.

Moving on to the administrative process, we believe that, regarding trade and investment disputes, when new rules or regulations are being considered, the text of the Protocol should include an explicit mandate that hearings be held and that interested parties have the right to advance notice of such hearings, along with the right to appear and give comments on the proposed changes. The Protocol should also require that records of the rulemaking hearing be published by MOFTEC and that new rules and regulations be accompanied by documents explaining the rationale behind them and their implications for future business activities. Consideration should also be given to putting teeth into the existing language, which mandates that China enforce only "those laws, regulations and other measures pertaining to or affecting trade in goods, services, TRIPs or the control of foreign exchange that are published."[23] WTO-member governments might be given the right to bring a case against the PRC if its domestic businesses were found guilty of an infraction for which there existed no previous or known regulation. Although there exists no truly satisfactory method for dealing with the normative documents, such a provision would force the Chinese to defend themselves in WTO-proceeding actions that are not covered by public laws or regulations. While individual judgments using secret normative documents might not rise to the level of a government-backed WTO complaint, certainly a pattern of such judgments would create a powerful case for violation of WTO obligations, and hence retaliation.[24]

Rules governing administrative adjudication should be more explicitly stated in the Protocol, and they should apply regardless of the venue chosen for the pursuit of the complaint—arbitration, current court system, or the special courts proposed in this volume. First, the right of a hearing on the record by the aggrieved or affected party should be written into the agreement, as should provisions for notice, right of counsel, and other safeguards to ensure that the rights of foreign businesses and investors are protected. In addition, consideration should be given to establishing some deadlines for prompt decisions and to introducing some standard of evidence, possibly a "reasonable, probative, and substantial standard": that is, in Western terms, the level of evidence used by a reasonable person in arriving at a decision. (This is a minimum standard, below that of "clear, unequivocal, and convincing.") As for what is possibly of greatest import at this stage of China's legal development, the Protocol should require that the administrative or court decision be published immediately and that it include a complete discussion, with citations to Chinese or WTO law and regulations, of the reasons behind the conclusion reached by the tribunal.

Questions also remain concerning appeals from initial-agency or court decisions. The Chinese legal system is multilayered, and there is a blurring of legislative, administrative, and judicial functions within and among agencies. For this reason, the Protocol should flesh out in some detail—with specific reference to the legal and institutional situation in China—how the mandate will be carried out regarding the matter of keeping appeal tribunals independent from the original administrative agency. What are the criteria for independence?

In summary, we advocate that a bare-bones set of procedures ensuring basic due process be written into the terms of accession. Certainly, these provisions do not include the full-blown additional trappings now in the U.S. Administrative Procedures Act. We do not think it possible or appropriate, for instance, to attempt to limit ex parte discussions, although admittedly these constitute a significant problem for China. Nor do we suggest Sunshine provisions for open meetings, or a Freedom of Information Act, or rules for evidence gathering or subpoena power. These provisions constitute only the bare minimum necessary to ensure fairness for foreign entities in trade and investment disputes—and from the Chinese perspective, a bare minimum to deflect expected criticism regarding the biased and arbitrary nature of their administrative law system.

A Note on Competition Policy and Private Restraints of Trade

Recently, an important new study of the experience of foreign investors in China was published by Daniel Rosen, of the Institute for International Economics. Although Rosen is generally optimistic about the prospects for increased foreign direct investment under the aegis of an ever more sophisticated and pragmatic system of commercial law, he warns that in many regions state ownership is in danger of being replaced by private collusion and anticompetitive practices between local firms—and sometimes between local firms and new foreign investors—to the exclusion of outside firms, both foreign and domestic. Rosen strongly recommends that the United States assume the lead in negotiating an agreement on competition-policy issues with the Chinese, although he takes a flexible position regarding the forum in which such an agreement could be achieved—bilateral, regional, or multilateral.[25] The last could be in the form of a Shanghai Round, to precede a new, multilateral Millennium Round.

In responding to this proposal, we will first support a statement that Rosen wrote in passing but that we consider worthy of being raised to a central principle: "It is important that this not be construed as raising the bar to Chinese (WTO) accession."[26] Although there are certainly legitimate issues to raise with the Chinese leaders, U.S. trade negotiators must also accept at least two realities concerning prospects for any kind of supranational agreement on competition policy.

First, there is little agreement among developing and developed countries alike about the content—and the timing—of competition-policy negotiations, whether in the Asia Pacific Economic Cooperation (APEC) forum or in the WTO. Rosen cites the examples of Japan's automobile and photographic film markets as illustrative of a system that is lax regarding private anticompetitive acts. Fair enough, but there is no evidence that Japan—or any other nation—is ready to accept U.S. principles of antitrust policies in bilateral, regional, or multilateral forums. Second, ironically, it is U.S. officials, led by our Justice Department, who have adamantly opposed any move toward an internationalization of rules for private competitive practices. They argue that other nations are either misguided in their policies or, in the case of many developing countries, possess legal systems too rudimentary to encompass rules for competition policy. In the end, while acknowledging that Rosen has raised a legitimate issue, we fail to see how his specific recommendations can be implemented within the foreseeable future.

5

虎

A Proposed Review Mechanism for Transition Economies

The most obvious vehicle for handling the complex issues associated with transition economies and the WTO is the Trade Policy Review Mechanism (TPRM). This procedural mechanism was established in 1989 to provide WTO members with unbiased information about the trade policies and practices of other members.

TPRM as It Stands Now

Originally created as an experiment, the TPRM was formally incorporated into the newly established WTO in the January 1995 Marrakesh Agreement at the conclusion of the Uruguay Round. The Marrakesh Agreement describes the function of the TPRM as follows:

> The objectives of the TPRM are to contribute to improved adherence by all WTO Members to rules, disciplines and commitments made under the Multilateral Trade Agreements and, where applicable, the Plurilateral Agreements, and hence to the smooth functioning of the multilateral trading system, by achieving greater transparency in, and understanding of, the trade policies and practices of Members. . . . [The TPRM] is not intended to serve as a basis for the enforcement of specific obligations under the Agreements,

or for dispute settlement procedures, or to impose new policy commitments on Members.[1]

To carry out the TPRM's policy-review mission, the Trade Policy Review Body (TPRB), composed of all members of the WTO, was created to oversee the reviews. A staff unit separate from the WTO Secretariat, the Trade Policy Review Division (TPRD), assumed the tasks of assembling and analyzing the information. Since 1989 the TPRM has conducted more than eighty trade policy reviews, covering more than sixty countries.[2]

Under current practices, the interval between reviews depends on the relative importance of the country to world trade. Thus, the United States, the European Union, Canada, and Japan are reviewed every two years; sixteen member-countries ranking next in their quantity of trade are reviewed every four years; other members are reviewed every six years—although some of the least developed countries may go longer without scrutiny.

Once a nation has been selected for review, the WTO Secretariat sends out a detailed questionnaire regarding its trade laws, regulations, and practices. That step is followed by one or more visits from the Secretariat staff, who meet with government officials, business leaders, consumer and other nongovernmental organizations, and private research and academic institutions. The staff prepares a preliminary report based on its own analysis and on the country report, stemming from the questionnaire. The staff report is followed by a meeting between the TPRD (or those members of the WTO who choose to participate in this particular review) and representatives from the government of the country under review. Often this meeting includes quite sharp exchanges between TPRD members and the government representatives. After the meeting, the TPRD prepares a final report that encompasses the initial Secretariat report, the country's self-report, and the minutes of the meeting.

The key document for the entire process is the Secretariat's independent assessment of the trade policies and practices of the country under review. The TPRM is still experimenting with different formats, and its reports vary in emphasis, but the standard organization consists of a four-chapter structure that includes the following contents:[3]

Chapter One—The Economic Environment. This chapter is an analysis of the country's macroeconomic policies, economic outlook, recent domestic and trade performance, and, often, its investment climate and policy.

Chapter Two—Trade Policy Regime: Framework and Objectives. Here the formal organizational and trade-policy objectives are described. They include the legal and regulatory framework that underlies trade and investment policy, the role of particular institutions, participation and obligations undertaken in the WTO, participation in regional or bilateral arrangements, and current trade disputes and settlements.

Chapter Three—Trade Policies and Practices by Measure. This is generally the most important and informative chapter in the report. Divided into import and export actions and policies, it describes and analyzes in detail the major protectionist policies and trade barriers currently in effect. On the import side, the report includes such topics as tariffs, import licenses, import quotas, import cartels, countertrade, government procurement, state-owned enterprises, antidumping measures, safeguards, and local-content schemes. On the export side, topics may include export licensing, export cartels, export subsidies, tax concessions, export finance and promotion, and export performance requirements. This chapter also contains important sections on the nation's intellectual-property and competition-policy regimes.

Chapter Four—Trade Policies and Practices by Sector. In this chapter, industrial and sectoral trade and investment policies are evaluated, usually under large headings such as agriculture, mining, energy, manufacturing, and services. The relatively new services section is of increasing length and importance.

The TPRM is a work in progress, still searching for the correct mixture of topics and breadth and depth of analysis. A recent evaluation of the process, however, argued that trade policy reviews "have matured from what were at first largely descriptive catalogs of countries' protectionist measures into more thorough, incisive and analytical surveys of trade policy and practices."[4] At the same time, Donald Keesing, who studied the program, concluded that substantial improvements are required in the quality and scope of the TPRMs. He cited the following needs: to take a longer-term perspective in evaluating current practices; to be more skeptical and critical of the actual effect of claimed liberalization; to overcome the optimistic bias that colors many reviews; to attempt some quantification of the costs of protection and protective nontariff barriers; and to evaluate national policies in the light of larger multilateral issues, such as the slow pace of textile and agricultural liberalization.[5]

A number of commentators have been much more critical of the TPRM reviews than is Keesing.[6] They argue that the reviewers, composed of WTO Secretariat staff, do not have the independence to deliver blunt and critical assessments of national trade policies and practices. Some have also suggested that outside reviewers be recruited to relieve the pressure on the Secretariat—pressure driven both by limited resources and by attacks from constituent WTO members. If the proposals recommended in this volume are adopted, the need for hard-hitting, candid opinions will be even more urgent. We therefore agree with those who argue that the current TPRM process should become more rigorous and that reviewers should be given more freedom to criticize those current protectionist practices that violate the letter and spirit of WTO rules. We also endorse a strengthening of the resources and staff of the WTO Secretariat.

Proposals for Combining Nonmarket Economies and the TPRM

For several reasons, we advocate using the China WTO accession process as the basis for establishing accession procedures for all the fifteen or twenty nations in transition from Communist command-economy states to market economies, rather than treating each on a case-by-case basis. As we have seen, the substantive and procedural slaloms that must be traversed on the road to membership are similar for these countries, and could be dealt with more efficiently through a common process. The resources of the WTO are already stretched. Why not consolidate where possible the duties and responsibilities of the Secretariat? Furthermore, establishing a common set of procedures and substantive rules for transition into the WTO would mitigate the candidate-nation's resentment and suspicion that rules of accession were being crafted only to penalize it, or even to thwart its pursuit of membership. This is particularly true for China, and may be expected for Russia as well.

It seems inevitable that the Chinese accession negotiations will lead through a bewildering and complex maze of interim deadlines and weigh stations, to be navigated before China is accorded full WTO membership. A major task of the TPRM bodies overseeing Chinese accession should be the evaluation of China's performance in meeting these deadlines and any progressive new obligations—along with fashioning penalties and remedies should the PRC fail to fulfill the terms of the final Protocol.

In recommending that the TPRM be adapted and expanded to include oversight of the nonmarket-economy (NME) accession process, the authors make the following arguments.[7] First, the central questions raised in the reviews—with some amending, reordering, and expanding—represent exactly the kind of information that will be needed to facilitate the progressive integration of the other NMEs into the World Trade Organization. Further, melding the format and the substantive agenda in the reviews with the accession process would place both the existing WTO members and the proposed new members on an equal footing in assessment of WTO membership-obligation fulfillment. Again, this step would lessen China's suspicions that it might be accorded a unique second-class citizenship in perpetuity.

Obviously, some changes would be necessary in order to combine the TPRM with a more general accession process for the other NMEs. Because the regular TPRM process will continue to operate, a subcommittee of the Trade Policy Review Body should be established to deal exclusively with NME accessions. Clearly, it would include the major trading members—the European Union, Japan, Canada, and the United States—plus other countries that would volunteer for the responsibility. The authors also recommend a change in the timing of the TPRM reviews to reflect the new priorities for the WTO and the limited resources available from the Secretariat. For the next decade at least, integration of the NMEs will remain a major challenge for the multilateral system; thus, the TPRM should concentrate its reviews on these nations as they enter the WTO. Specifically, the NMEs should receive top priority and be reviewed every two years, while the current two-year reviews for the United States, European Union, Canada, and Japan should be stretched out to four or six years. This change reflects another reality: that, whatever their flaws, the trading practices and institutions of these countries do not change very much over short periods of time, and hence little would be lost in terms of trade liberalization. It is true that small WTO members, who do not have the resources to monitor the complex trade policies of larger nations, utilize the TPRM to protect their interests. But we do not believe that the slippage from four, or even six, years would greatly affect their ability to challenge serious infractions of WTO rules by the larger nations.

We recognize that our proposal would necessitate some trade-offs and some changes in philosophy. The Trade Policy Review Mechanism, and in particular the Trade Policy Review Body subcommittee that would oversee NME transitions, would have to take on a more activist role in place of its current "external audit" function. The subcommittee's role in presiding over the separate safeguards and anti-dumping actions we have suggested for NMEs, however, would still not include a dispute-settlement function. That function would continue to be met through the regular WTO process. The major new responsibilities would be the oversight of the market-access pledges and the creation of penalties for failure to meet these deadlines.

6

虎

Conclusions

One Chinese commentator recently remarked, "To not reform is to wait for death, to reform is to look for death" (*bu gaizao shi deng si, gao gaizao shi zhao si*).[1] We are not so pessimistic, but we recognize that China faces severe difficulties in restructuring its economy in the years ahead. This process will be all the more difficult in the context of the Asian economic crisis afflicting the region. Already in the late 1990s there is evidence that China's economy is deteriorating and the reforms are beginning to stall.[2] As noted in the introduction to this volume, we do not believe that China's accession to the WTO will prove to be a panacea for the problems it faces. Nor do we believe that China should accede to the WTO at all costs. The Chinese must commit themselves to meaningful sectoral liberalization and must improve their administrative and legal systems.

The recommendations in this study call for major shifts in underlying attitudes and specific positions, both for China and for the key negotiators of the United States and the European Union. If China continues to view all transparency and market-access demands as evidence of a "conspiracy" to deny it a rightful place in world economic affairs, then its worthwhile goal of WTO membership will only be delayed and ultimately frustrated.

China has much to gain by softening its stance and compromising its negotiating positions on the key sticking points. The PRC will need a more stable and predictable world market for its exports and a domestic legal system that is conducive to vital foreign direct investment. To attain this stability and predictability, membership in the WTO is an indispensable prerequisite. As former WTO Director General Renato Ruggiero asserted, "China's economic relations with the world are simply too large and too pervasive to manage effectively through a maze of arbitrary, shifting, and unstable bilateral deals."[3]

Membership in the WTO will allow China to attain three concrete goals: permanent assurance of nondiscrimination, through most-favored-nation status; insulation against unilateral trade sanctions, through participation in a legally binding dispute-settlement system; and a voice in establishing new trading rules in the future, in areas such as the environment, investment, and competition policy.

It will be important for U.S. and other Western leaders to convince the Chinese that the legal and economic reforms being demanded as the price of WTO membership are in their own economic interest—and not onerous obligations pressed upon them to undermine their economic progress. As Douglas North and Robert Thomas have said in their influential thesis regarding the forces behind the burst of economic growth in the West over the past four centuries, "The development of an efficient economic organization in Western Europe accounts for the rise of the West. . . . Efficient economic organization is the key to growth." They explain the reason for this:

> Growth will simply not occur unless the existing economic organization is efficient. Individuals must be lured by incentives to undertake the socially desirable activities. Some mechanism must be devised to bring social and private rates of return into closer parity. . . . A discrepancy between private and social benefits or costs means that some third party or parties, without their consent, will receive some of the benefits or incur some of the costs. Such a difference occurs whenever property rights are poorly defined, or not enforced.[4]

Of interest also for the Chinese will be the fact that, as North and Thomas point out, "Karl Marx and Adam Smith both subscribed to this view. They both saw successful growth as dependent on the development of efficient property rights. Their followers in the main have forgotten this."[5]

For the West, a daunting reality hangs on the outcome of the negotiations for Chinese WTO membership. China will set an important precedent for the way the WTO deals with the numerous other nonmarket economies, such as Russia, which remain outside the system. Regardless of the particular market-access agreements reached, it is important that compliance with WTO rules and principles be evaluated on the basis of the process by which trade is conducted— not on the actual volume of trade between member-nations. Those advocating a managed-trade position, whereby one evaluates China's liberalization by the degree to which it imports products, are really mercantilists in disguise. Greg Mastel, for example, laments on the one hand that China is a closed market, but on the other goes on to state, "What is worse, U.S. exports to China have not kept pace with those of Japan and Europe."[6] The contradiction in Mastel's logic should be clear: if Japan and Europe are increasing exports to China, then the market is not as closed as Mastel would suggest.

In the end, for all the difficulties and dangers that full membership for China entails for the multilateral trading system, China—and Russia and the other transition economies—must be accommodated and integrated if the WTO aspires to retain its claim and status as a global economic and legal force. As John Jackson perceptively wrote some years ago, "It will be very difficult in the long run to deny membership in the GATT to any important nation of the world. Since the GATT is the principal world trading institution, strong arguments can be made that it must be a universal institution, for both political and economic reasons."[7] Economic institutions such as the WTO help promote dialogue between nations in stable and predictable ways. Such a dialogue has both political and economic ramifications. Politically, while it is overstating the case to suggest that the WTO will preserve peace in the world, WTO-like institutions can help diffuse economic tensions that might escalate into political conflicts. Moreover, it will allow countries to focus more directly on legitimate political differences by making moot the argument that some countries are intentionally trying to keep rising countries such as China from prospering economically. Economically, we have already seen how the WTO-led liberalization of economies has enhanced welfare in both developed and developing countries. Accession to the WTO will help China continue along the difficult path of reforming its economy into one governed increasingly by market forces and the rule of law—something that is in the interest of the entire world community.

虎

Notes

CHAPTER 1: INTRODUCTION

1. First, China promised to reduce average tariffs on more than 5,000 products, from corn and wheat to automobiles, semiconductors, and cellular phones. Second, and of even greater importance, Zhu agreed for the first time to major changes relating to services, including: (1) accession to the recently negotiated Financial Services and Telecommunications Agreements; (2) after a brief period, eliminating the ban on foreign investment in telecommunications, insurance, and banking companies; (3) eliminating geographic restrictions on the provision of insurance and banking services; (4) lifting a ban on foreign companies distributing foreign products and services, including wholesaling, and repair and maintenance services; and (5) comparable marketing-opening provisions in the audiovisual, professional-services, and travel-and-tourism sector. In high-technology sectors, the PRC will henceforth cease to demand that foreign companies share their technology as a condition of receiving licenses and contracts.

2. To be sure, we acknowledge our firm belief that nontrade related issues such as espionage and accidental bombings, while important in their own right, should have no place in the debate on China's accession to the WTO.

3. For a discussion on "hybrid" economies in the case of the PRC, see Victor Nee, "Organizational Dynamics of Market Transition: Hybrid Forms, Property Rights, and Mixed Economy in China," *Administrative Science Quarterly*, vol. 37, 1992, pp. 1–27.

4. "China Faces Huge Welfare Burden," *Financial Times*, April 14, 1999.

5. Quoted in James Harding, "Zhu Faces Opposition to WTO Entry," *Financial Times*, April 10–11, 1999.

6. *International Trade Reporter*, December 3, 1998, pp. 2070–71.

7. Bruce Stokes, "Almost Now-or-Never Time," *National Journal*, December 12, 1998, pp. 2948–49.

8. Chalmers Johnson, "Breaching the Great Wall," *American Prospect*, January-February 1997, p. 28.

9. Report by the Labor-Industry Coalition for International Trade, "Getting What We Bargained For: Industry Evaluates U.S. Enforcement of Trade Agreements to Gain Access to Foreign Markets," April 1998, p. 7.

10. Greg Mastel, "U.S. Trade Policy Toward China," *Washington Quarterly*, Winter 1996, p. 202.

11. With regard to the United States-Japan Semiconductor agreement, two leading economists have noted: "If the Semiconductor Agreement is an example of successful 'managed trade,' it is hard to know what might constitute a failure"; David C. Mowery and Nathan Rosenberg, "New Developments in U.S. Technology Policy: Implications for Competitiveness and International Trade Policy," *California Management Review*, vol. 32, Fall 1989, p. 113. Ironically, as Andrew Dick concludes, the agreement "has been extremely costly to U.S. customers and the U.S. semiconductor industry, and highly profitable to Japanese companies." Andrew Dick, *Industrial Policy and Semiconductors* (Washington, D.C.: AEI Press, 1995), p. 53.

12. Leah H. Haus, *Globalizing the GATT: The Soviet Union's Successor States, Eastern Europe, and the International Trading System* (Washington, D.C.: Brookings Institution Press, 1992), p. 62.

13. William Alford, "When Is China Paraguay? An Examination of the Application of the Antidumping and Countervailing Duty Laws of the United States to China and Other 'Nonmarket Economy' Nations," *Southern California Law Review*, vol. 61, 1987, p. 118.

CHAPTER 2: MAJOR NEGOTIATING ISSUES

1. See Thomas W. Robinson, "Interdependence in China's Foreign Relations," in Samuel S. Kim, ed., *China and the World*, 3rd edition (Boulder, Colo.: Westview Press, 1994), p. 193.

2. Peter Harrold, "China: Foreign Trade Reform—Now for the Hard Part," *Oxford Review of Economic Policy*, vol. 11, 1995, p. 135.

3. Mark A. Groombridge, "Is the Asian Flu Still Infectious? The Case of China," *Looking Ahead*, August 1998, pp. 21–24.

4. "U.S. Trade Official Says China Market Is Closed Tighter," *New York Times*, September 23, 1998.

5. Harrold, "Now for the Hard Part," p. 142.

6. "China Market Is Closed Tighter," *New York Times*.

7. Anne Krueger, *American Trade Policy: A Tragedy in the Making* (Washington, D.C.: AEI Press, 1995), p. 17.

8. Douglas A. Irwin, *Three Simple Principles of Trade Policy* (Washington, D.C.: AEI Press, 1996), pp. 26 and 18.

9. Nicholas R. Lardy, "China and the WTO," *Brookings Policy Brief*, no. 10, November 1996, pp. 2–3.

10. For a detailed documentation of this point, see Robert C. Feenstra, Wen Hai, Wing T. Woo, and Shunli Yao, "The U.S.-China Bilateral Trade Balance: Its Size and Determinants," National Bureau of Economic Research, Inc., working paper #6598, June 1998.

11. For a more detailed discussion on this point, see Harold K. Jacobson and Michael Oksenberg, *China's Participation in the IMF, the World Bank, and GATT* (Ann Arbor, Mich.: University of Michigan Press, 1990).

12. Ibid., p. 84. Access to markets in industrialized countries was particularly important given the tremendous growth in the PRC's textile industry at this time. As Minister of Textiles Hao Jianxiu argued, "Since the Third Plenum [December 1978] . . . the textile industry has enjoyed strong support from the state. . . . In the five years from 1977 through 1981, the output value, accumulation, and export foreign exchange value of the textile industry increased by 125 percent, 137 percent, and 148 percent, respectively." Hao Jianxiu, "Concentrate Forces to Accelerate Technical Transformation of the Textile Industry," *Renmin ribao*, January 12, 1983, in BBC, February 2, 1983.

13. We are grateful to Sarath Rajapatirana for clarifying this point.

14. Statement by Shen Jueren, deputy minister of foreign economic relations and trade, head of the Chinese delegation at the third session of the GATT working party on China; Geneva, Switzerland, April 26, 1988.

15. Ibid. For a broader discussion of this point, see Ya Qin, "China and GATT: Accession Instead of Resumption," *Journal of World Trade*, vol. 27, 1993, pp. 77–98.

16. J.E.D. McDonnell, "China's Move to Rejoin the GATT System: An Epic Transition," *World Economy*, vol. 10, 1987, pp. 331–50. See also Robert P. O'Quinn, "Integrating China into the World Economy," in Kim Holmes and James Przystup, eds., *Between Diplomacy and Deterrence* (Washington, D.C.: Heritage Foundation Press, 1997), p. 64. A little-used provision of WTO rules does allow a current member of the WTO, on a one-time basis, *not* to extend all benefits to new members.

17. Jeffrey L. Gertler, "The Process of China's Accession to the World Trade Organization," in Frederick M. Abbott, ed., *China in the World Trading System: Defining Principles of Engagement* (The Hague: Kluwer Law International, 1998), p. 68.

18. For a thorough review of this matter, see Alan S. Alexandroff, "Concluding China's Accession to the WTO: The U.S. Congress and Permanent Most-Favored-Nation Status for China," mimeo, 1998.

19. "China Faces Test of Resolve to Join Global Economy," *New York Times*, March 1, 1997, p. 14.

20. Bruce Stokes, "For a Change, Try Statesmanship," *National Journal*, May 30, 1998, p. 1253.

21. "Unfinished Business," *Far Eastern Economic Review*, December 17, 1998, p. 22.

22. See Mark A. Groombridge, "The Politics of Industrial Bargaining: The Restructuring of State-Owned Enterprises in the People's Republic of China, 1978 to 1996," Ph.D. dissertation, Columbia University, 1998.

23. Dorothy Solinger, "Despite Decentralization: Disadvantages, Dependence, and Ongoing Central Power in the Inland—The Case of Wuhan," *China Quarterly*, Winter 1996, p. 17.

24. "Coastal Areas Enter New Area," *Beijing Review*, April 29–May 5, 1996, p. 15.

25. Debates abound over the size and effect of extrabudgetary funds. Guo Zhenqian, the auditor general of the PRC, reported that extrabudgetary funds exceeded 200 billion yuan ($U.S. 24 billion) in 1995 alone, accounting for more than half of central budgetary revenues. "China Finds State Funds Diverted into Stocks," Reuters, July 4, 1996. Keun Lee argues that extrabudgetary funds "became a vast source of unproductive and redundant local investment and collective consumption and contributed to inflation." Keun Lee, *Chinese Firms and the State in Transition* (Armonk, N.Y.: M.E. Sharpe, Inc., 1991), p. 166. Solinger, while acknowledging the possible role of extrabudgetary funds, still finds the role of the central leadership to be significant in providing investment funds. Solinger, "The Case of Wuhan," particularly pp. 6–7.

26. World Bank, *China: Internal Market Development and Regulation* (Washington, D.C.: World Bank Press, 1994), pp. 47–48.

27. "Ningbo Bucks National Trend," *China Daily (Business Weekly)*, July 2–8, 1995, p. 5.

28. World Bank, *China: Foreign Trade Regime* (Washington, D.C.: World Bank Press, 1994), p. 249.

29. K. C. Fung, Lawrence Lau, and Joseph Lee, *U.S.-China Direct Investment Relations*, mimeo, 1998, p. 52.

30. Sarah Biddulph, "Legal System Transparency and Administrative Reform," mimeo, prepared for the China-WTO Accession Project, Washington, D.C., March 5–6, 1998, p. 5.

31. Like Mao Zedong, Deng Xiaoping had no qualms about purging his opponents. The purges of Hu Yaobang and Zhao Ziyang exemplify this.

32. Pitman B. Potter, *The Economic Contract Law of China: Legitimation and Contract Autonomy in the PRC* (Seattle, Wash.: University of Washington Press, 1992), p. 3. The economic contract law (ECL)—at least in theory—established legal rights for contracting parties, reduced the power of outside actors (party and government officials) to supervise and intervene in contract formation, and strengthened the enforceability of contracts through emphasis on judicially managed compulsory dispute resolution and monetary remedies for

nonperformance. The ECL was complemented in 1987 by a foreign economic contract law that established legal rules for contracts between Chinese and foreign businesses. For more details, see David A. Hayden, "The Role of Contract Law in Developing Chinese Legal Culture," *Hastings International and Comparative Law Review*, vol. 10, 1987, pp. 571–76.

33. Potter, *Economic Contract Law of China*, p. 13.

34. Ibid., p. 11.

35. Ibid., pp. 119–21.

36. Andrew Walder, "Property Rights and Stratification in Socialist Redistributive Economies," *American Sociological Review*, August 1992, p. 528.

37. David Granick, *Chinese State Enterprises* (Chicago: University of Chicago Press, 1990), p. 16.

38. "Column on Beijing's Efforts to Recentralize," *Hong Kong Hsin Pao*, June 3, 1994, in Foreign Broadcast Information Service-China (hereafter, FBIS-CHI), June 7, 1994, p. 30.

39. Jean Oi, "Rational Choices, Wealth, Power," in David Goodman and Beverly Hooper, eds., *China's Quiet Revolution* (New York: St. Martin's Press, 1994), pp. 72–73.

40. *Guangming Ribao*, January 4, 1994, in FBIS-CHI, January 14, 1994, p. 37.

41. *Fazhi Ribao*, March 7, 1993, p. 2, in FBIS-CHI, March 19, 1993, p. 48.

42. "State Council Approves Draft Revision to Rules," *China Daily*, September 26, 1998, p. 1.

43. Wang Haibo, "An Analysis of the Characteristics of Current Changes in Industrial Economic Returns," *Jingji Guanli*, no. 9, September 5, 1993, in FBIS-CHI, October 26, 1993, p. 35.

44. "Chinese Scramble for Assets in Ownership Chaos," Reuters, December 11, 1995.

45. Basic Instruments and Selected Documents, "Text of the General Agreement," Article XVII (1) b, p. 27.

46. Barry Naughton, "China's Emergence and Prospects as a Trading Nation," *Brookings Papers on Economic Activity*, 2, 1996, p. 302.

47. Peter Harrold, "China: Foreign Trade Reform—Now for the Hard Part," *Oxford Review of Economic Policy*, vol. 11, 1995, p. 137.

48. "Market Access and Protocol Commitments," United States Trade Representative Office Press Release, April 1999, available on www.ustr.gov, p. 6.

49. "China Issues Trade Licenses, Breaks Monopoly," *Agence France Presse*, January 4, 1999.

50. United States-China Business Council, *China and the WTO: Critical Issues and Objectives*, June 1998, p. 3.

51. "Exports Held Up by Red Tape at Foreign Trade Ministry," *Xinhua*, November 25, 1979, in BBC, December 4, 1979.

52. Will Martin and Christian Bach, "State Trading in China," in Thomas

Cottier and Petros Mavroides, eds., *State Trading in the Twenty-First Century* (Ann Arbor, Mich.: University of Michigan Press, 1998).

53. "Market Access and Protocol Commitments," United States Trade Representative Office Press Release, April 1999, available on www.ustr.gov.

54. See Franz Schurmann, particularly chapter 4, for a good discussion on this process, in *Ideology and Organization in Communist China* (Berkeley, Calif.: University of California Press, 1966).

55. "China Slowly Modernizing Its Massive Coal Industry," *Japanese Economic Newswire*, July 16, 1995.

56. Zheng Xinfa, "*Jinnian guoyou qiye gaige you na xie xin jucuo? Fang guojia tigaiwei fuzhuren Wang Shiyuan*," *Gaige yu lilun*, March 1995, pp. 3–5.

57. Personal interview by Mark A. Groombridge with Tang Haibin, division chief, Economic Regulations Bureau, State Economic and Trade Commission, New York City, September 14, 1995. One manager spoke of mentally ill workers in a camera factory actually spending all day sitting in the commons. Although they are unable to work, they have nowhere else to go, given the condition of mental hospitals. Guangdong Province, Guangzhou, June 21, 1995.

58. Zheng, "*Jinnian guoyou qiye gaige?*" p. 4.

59. *Laodongbu zonghe jihuasi he goujia tongjiju shehui jisi, 1990 Laodong tongji nianjian* (Beijing: *Zhongguo laodong chubanshe*, 1991), p. 498.

60. Ibid., p. vii.

61. Cao Hongzhi and Cao Yang, "*Shixing chanquan zhidu gaige—jianli xiandai qiye zhidu*," *Gongye jishu jingji*, vol. 14, 1995, pp. 1–3.

62. Liu Zhaobin, "*Jianli xin tizhi de yiwei dashi: peiyu he fazhan chanquan shangchang*," *Zhongguo tizhi gaige*, vol. 93, September 1993, pp. 28–29.

63. Jiang Yifan, "Without State Enterprises, There Is No Socialism," *Zhenli de zhuiqui*, September 11, 1993, in *Journal of Public Research Services* (hereafter *JPRS*), November 23, 1993, p. 9.

64. Leroy P. Jones and Edward S. Mason, *Public Enterprise in Less Developed Countries* (Cambridge, U.K.: Cambridge University Press, 1982), chapter 2.

65. "Market Access Key to China's Entry," *China Daily* (Business Weekly Supplement), November 19, 1997, p. 1.

66. Cheng Zhiping, "Improving the Business Operations of Large and Medium-Sized State Enterprises," *Zhongguo Wujia*, March 17, 1992, pp. 2–5; in *JPRS*, July 1, 1992, p. 24. See also "China: State Enterprises Lead Reform Efforts," *China Daily*, September 15, 1995. Finally, see "Progress in Reform State-Owned Enterprises," *Beijing Review*, June 17–23, 1996, pp. 15–16.

67. "Li Explains Plenum's Development Plan," *China Daily*, October 6, 1995, p. 3.

68. "NPC Deputies Discuss Reform of State-Owned Enterprises," *Xinhua*, March 9, 1995.

69. East Asia Analytical Unit, Department of Foreign Affairs and Trade of

Australia, *China Embraces the Market* (Barton: Commonwealth of Australia, 1997), p. 336.

70. "China Aims to Sell Off 90,000 State Firms," Reuters, July 14, 1996.

71. Ibid.

72. Li Tieying, "Fifteen Years of Reform for State-Owned Enterprises," *Beijing Review*, vol. 38, January 9–15, 1995, p. 17.

73. "China to Maintain Socialist Economy, Open Up to Foreign Capital," *Agence France Presse*, December 18, 1998.

74. "Dominant Role of State Enterprises Will Expand in Market Conditions," *Renmin Ribao*, November 21, 1995, in BBC, December 20, 1995.

75. Yang Yongzheng, "China's WTO Membership: What's at Stake?" *World Economy*, November 1996, p. 663.

76. "U.S. Trade Imbalance with Beijing Called Evidence of China's Closed Market," *International Trade Reporter*, vol. 14, February 5, 1997, p. 222.

77. "Grasp the Opportunity and Revitalize the Pillar Industries," *Renmin Ribao*, March 29, 1994, p. 2, in FBIS-CHI, April 5, 1994, p. 21. In Shanghai, for example, "China's largest economic center has formed pillar industries of its automobile, telecommunications, iron and steel, power station equipment, petrochemicals and electric appliance sectors. . . . The total sales volume of these industries last year [1993] amounted to 106.7 billion yuan ($U.S. 8.5 billion), accounting for 38.2 percent of the city's total. The proportions of light and heavy industries are 45.2 and 54.8, thanks to the adjustment and approaches of the production system of the world's economically developed countries." In "Shanghai Forms Six Pillar Industries," *Xinhua*, May 26, 1994.

78. "Foreign Funds Usage," *China Daily*, January 10, 1998, p. 4.

79. Dorothy Solinger, *China's Transition from Socialism* (Armonk, N.Y.: M.E. Sharpe, Inc., 1993), p. 3.

80. "Price Law to Regulate Market-Pricing System," *China Daily*, January 10, 1998, p. 4.

81. "China Refuses to Reopen WTO Negotiations with US," *The Financial Times*, May 27, 1999.

82. "Market Access and Protocol Commitments," United States Trade Representative Office Press Release, April 1999, available on www.ustr.gov, p. 6.

83. Ibid., p. 7.

84. World Bank, *China Foreign Trade Regime* (Washington, D.C.: World Bank, 1994), p. 57.

85. "China Slashes Tariff Rate Once Again," *Beijing Review*, December 1–7, 1997, p. 18.

86. Yang, "What's at Stake?" *World Economy*, p. 664.

87. Thomas P. Bernstein, "Ideology and Rural Reform," in Arthur Lewis Rosenbaum, ed., *State and Society in China: The Consequences of Reform* (Boulder, Colo.: Westview Press, 1992), pp. 160–61.

88. "Market Access and Protocol Commitments," United States Trade Representative Office Press Release, April 1999, available on www.ustr.gov.

89. Ibid.

90. Ibid.

91. "China Agrees to Meeting on Wheat Fungus Dispute," *International Trade Reporter*, vol. 15, July 1, 1998, p. 1130.

92. "Market Access and Protocol Commitments," United States Trade Representative Office Press Release, April 1999, available on www.ustr.gov.

93. "Chinese Premier Urges Cooperation in Telecom Sector," *China Daily*, September 4, 1997.

94. "China Curbs Foreign Role in Telecoms," *Financial Times*, December 14, 1998, p. 4.

95. "China Telecom Market Keeps Foreigners at Bay," *Agence France Presse*, August 26, 1997.

96. "China Telecom Develops Apace," *Beijing Review*, May 4–10, 1998, p. 21.

97. "Telecom Market Keeps Foreigners at Bay," *Agence France Presse*.

98. "China: Plea to PM on Telecoms," *Financial Times*, February 26, 1999.

99. The first of the two quoted passages originally appeared in the newspaper *Beijing Youth News*. The second originally appeared in an economic journal and was written by sociologist Wang Hansong. It was later reported on radio by the central news agency *Xinhua*. Both were reprinted in "Chinese Press Says State Telecom Monopoly Hampers Growth," *Agence France Presse*, September 5, 1997.

100. "China Ready to Open Market to Telecoms," *Journal of Commerce*, January 6, 1999, p. A3.

101. "China's Mobile Phone Network to Triple by Year 2000," *China Daily*, August 21, 1997.

102. "Comeback Kid," *Far East Economic Review*, September 3, 1998, p. 11.

103. "China Telecom Develops Apace," *Beijing Review*. It is noteworthy that the PRC government has attempted to regulate the Internet in other ways as well, relating to social and political goals. As Minister Wu noted, "The Chinese government is always of the view that it must take advantage of the Internet while eliminating its shortcomings." China "adopts measures against anything that is detrimental to the country's security and that goes against the country's traditions." Beijing blocks foreign-news, pornographic, and anti-Beijing sites. But the government is finding the Internet increasingly difficult to control. "The Chinese government is trying to make China's situation better known through the Internet. It spreads facts about China through the Internet so that misunderstandings about China can be corrected." In "Telecom Market Keeps Foreigners at Bay," *Agence France Presse*.

104. "'Flexible' Attitude Urged in WTO Talks," *China Daily*, July 9, 1998, p. 1.

105. Mark A. Groombridge, "Dragon Droop: Why China's Economic Future Might Be Less Spectacular Than You Think," *American Enterprise*, vol. 9, July–August 1998, p. 35.

106. Barry Naughton, "China's Emergence and Prospects as a Trading Nation," *Brookings Papers on Economic Activity*, 2, 1996, p. 295.

107. "Business Leaders Are Torn on China Talks," *Wall Street Journal*, April 12, 1999, p. A10.

108. A useful overview and much of the data in this section draw from Liu Guangxi, "Progress in Opening Up Service Sector," *Beijing Review*, September 7–13, 1998, pp. 16–21.

109. "Opening China's Financial Market in a Planned Way," *Beijing Review*, November 23–29, 1998, p. 21.

110. "Financial Sector to Be Further Opened," *Beijing Review*, December 21–27, 1998, p. 4.

111. For a more detailed discussion on this matter, see Mark A. Groombridge, "The Political Economy of Intellectual Property Rights Protection in the People's Republic of China," in Clarisa Long, ed., *Intellectual Property Rights in Emerging Markets* (Washington, D.C.: AEI Press, forthcoming).

112. Michael N. Schlesinger, "A Sleeping Giant Awakens: The Development of Intellectual Property Law in China," *Journal of Chinese Law*, vol. 9, 1995, p. 95.

113. David C. Buxbaum, "Enforcement of IP Rights: Courts and Administrative Organizations," in Michael Fawlk, ed., *Intellectual Property Protection in China* (Hong Kong: Asia Law and Practice, Ltd., 1996), p. 40.

114. "Patent Law to Be Revised," *China Daily*, April 14, 1998, p. 1.

115. "What Has China Done to Protect Intellectual Property Rights?" *Chinese Embassy Web Page* (www.china-embassy.org/Cgi-Bin), June 9, 1998.

116. Wang Ping, director, Beijing Municipality, Haidian District Commerce Bureau, "IPR and Protective Counter-Policies for High-Technology Enterprise," *Beijing Keji Ribao*, September 30, 1997, p. 8, in "China: Official on Policy to Protect High-Tech IPR," in FBIS-CHI, December 17, 1997.

117. Peter Feng, *Intellectual Property in China* (Hong Kong: Sweet and Maxwell Asia, 1997), p. 14.

118. Wang, "IPR and Protective Counter-Policies."

119. "Patent Law," *China Daily*.

120. "Unfinished Business," *Far Eastern Economic Review*, December 17, 1998, p. 22.

CHAPTER 3: NONMARKET ECONOMIES AND THE WTO

1. John H. Jackson, *World Trade and the Law of GATT* (New York: Bobbs Merrill Co., 1969), p. 334. More generally, see Jackson's treatment of state trad-

ing companies in John H. Jackson, *The World Trading System* (Cambridge, Mass.: MIT Press, 1989), chapter 13.

2. Jackson, *World Trade and the Law of GATT.*

3. Ibid.

4. P. D. McKenzie, "China's Application to the GATT: State Trading Companies and the Problem of Market Access," *Journal of World Trade*, vol. 24, 1990, pp. 137–39; Will Martin and Christian Bach, "State Trading in China," in Thomas Cottier and Petros Mavroides, eds., *State Trading in the Twenty-First Century* (Ann Arbor, Mich.: University of Michigan Press, 1998).

5. Leah H. Haus, *Globalizing the GATT: The Soviet Union's Successor States, Eastern Europe, and the International Trading System* (Washington, D.C.: Brookings Institution Press, 1992), p. 36. For a full description of Polish, Romanian, and Hungarian experiences, see chapter 3. See also Jackson, *World Trading System*, chapter 13; and J. M. Reuland, "GATT and State Trading Companies," *Journal of World Trade Law*, vol. 9, 1975, pp. 318–39.

6. Haus, *Globalizing the GATT*, p. 33.

7. Polish imports from contracting parties fluctuated wildly: they were 9.3 percent in 1969; 7.9 percent in 1970; 18 percent in 1971; 48.9 percent in 1972; 65.3 percent in 1973; 41.8 percent in 1974; 15.1 percent in 1975; and 11.4 percent in 1976. Ibid., p. 61.

8. The export-import connection stemmed from the fact that Poland was expected to expend foreign-exchange capital gained by exports for imports at exactly the same rate. This circumstance obviated the original reason to adopt external orientation: that is, for the accumulation of foreign-exchange capital. McKenzie, "China's Application to the GATT," p. 142.

9. Haus, *Globalizing the GATT*, p. 42.

10. McKenzie, "China's Application to the GATT," p. 143.

11. "Closer Yet on US-China Trade Agreement," *Washington Trade Daily*, April 29, 1999, pp. 2–3.

12. "Special Report: Confidential Draft Protocol Proposes Unlimited China Safeguard," *Inside U.S. Trade*, January 27, 1995, p. 10; hereinafter cited as the Protocol.

13. China has bitterly protested the use of surrogate countries for determining costs and prices, arguing that this practice results in unfair and inaccurate comparisons with the Chinese market. The Chinese point out that India and Pakistan, often chosen as surrogates, both have more expensive raw materials than China has. And highly developed countries such as Norway, Austria, and France have also on occasion served as surrogates, resulting in equally distorted price calculations.

It is useful here to comment on an early and provocative study of U.S. antidumping laws and nonmarket economies: William Alford's "When Is China Paraguay? An Examination of the Application of the Antidumping and Countervailing Duty Laws of the United States to China and Other 'Nonmarket Economy' Nations," *Southern California Law Review*, vol. 61, 1987, pp. 79–135.

Although this study was written before the passage of the 1988 Trade Act, Alford's skewering of the hapless attempts of U.S. officials to define the characteristics of market and nonmarket economies remains instructive today. He points out that, "Adam Smith notwithstanding, there are no major segments of any national economy here or abroad operating as pure markets, wholly responsive only to supply and demand." Thus, in antidumping and in subsidies, in both GATT codes and U.S. law, "we are dealing . . . with differences of degree rather than with simple, sharp distinctions of kind, for neither has been able to provide convincing and consistent definitions of market and nonmarket economy behavior."

Alford goes on to argue that while China may evolve toward a Western market economy, it also may stubbornly remain a planned society, with large elements of coordinated national development: "For although the Chinese have embraced part of the rhetoric and even some of the forms that we might associate with a market economy, their use of that vocabulary and of those forms suggests a very different conception of the nature, place, and ultimate objective of market forces in their society. . . . Chinese officials have been quick to point out that their increased reliance upon market forces is best understood as taking place within the context of central planning, with the ultimate goal of energizing and supplementing the planning process in order to further largely centrally directed national development."

Finally, Alford contends that GATT itself has never lived up to free-market principles and therefore that GATT should accommodate China and other transition economies, even though they may never become true market economies. "A range of GATT provisions reveals that . . . departures from the path of the market are not the aberrations that some commentators have suggested. . . . GATT, ultimately, is more appropriately understood and defended as a political institution that expresses agreement among the major trading states as to acceptable trade practices, rather than as an economic institution embodying the undistilled principles of hard science." In Alford, "When Is China Paraguay?" pp. 130–31.

We find ourselves both strongly agreeing and disagreeing with aspects of Alford's challenging analysis and conclusions. We fully agree that the United States and the European Union have failed to come up with acceptable standards for dealing with NMEs regarding dumping and countervailing duties. In this volume we suggest less rigid policies that would accommodate the market evolution in China and in other NMEs. But we disagree with Alford's claims that, first, one cannot distinguish between market and nonmarket practices and policies, and second, that the WTO can be expanded to include fifteen to twenty NMEs, including Russia and China, without major reforms in those nations' economic systems. It is true that the United States and European Union have exploited trade-remedy policies for rent-seeking national industries; but for all their shortcomings, both the United States and the European Union have evolved over the past four decades away from government subsidy and regulation, toward increased privatization. The WTO is in effect an economic institution—its foundations, in any case, are based on economic principles—and it would be destroyed by allowing China and Russia to become members without substantial revision of their current industrial, trade, and investment policies.

14. Peter D. Ehrenhaft, "U.S. Policy on Imports from Economies in Transition," in Peter D. Ehrenhaft, Brian Vernon Hindley, Constantine Michalopoulos, and L. Alan Winters, eds., *Policies on Imports from Economies in Transition: Two Case Studies*, Studies of Economies in Transition, no. 22 (Washington, D.C.: World Bank, 1997), p. 25.

15. Judith H. Bello, Alan F. Holmer, and Jeremy O. Preiss, "Searching for 'Bubbles of Capitalism': Application of the U.S. Antidumping and Countervailing Duty Laws to Reforming Nonmarket Economies," *George Washington University Journal of International Law and Economics*, vol. 25, 1992, p. 689. See also Gary Horlick and Shannon Shuman, "Nonmarket Economy Trends and U.S. Antidumping / Countervailing Duty Laws," *International Law Journal*, vol. 18, 1984, pp. 807–29.

16. Bello, Holmer, and Preiss, "Searching for 'Bubbles of Capitalism.'"

17. Sanghan Wang, "U.S. Trade Laws Concerning Nonmarket Economies Revisited for Fairness and Consistency," *Emory International Law Review*, vol. 10, 1996, p. 637.

18. This section is derived from ibid., pp. 594–655, and from Robert H. Lantz, "The Search for Consistency: Treatment of Nonmarket Economies in Transition under United States Antidumping and Contervailing Duty Laws," *American University Journal of International Law and Policy*, vol. 10, 1995, pp. 993–1073, especially pp. 1036–50. Even before the 1988 act, Commerce Department officials had toyed with the idea of a bubbles-of-capitalism approach, according to Robert Herzstein in a personal communication with the authors, March 1, 1999. The cases referred to were *Chrome-plated Lug Nuts from the PRC*, 55 Federal Register 49548, Department of Commerce, 1990; and *Oscillating Fans and Ceiling Fans from the PRC*, 55 Federal Register 49320, Department of Commerce, 1990.

19. Bello, Holmer, and Preiss, "Searching for 'Bubbles of Capitalism,'" p. 718, fn. 287. See also Greg Mastel, *Antidumping Laws and the U.S. Economy* (Armonk, N.Y.: M.E. Sharpe, 1998), p. 55.

20. Wang, "U.S. Trade Laws," p. 644. From a purely theoretical basis, the Commerce Department is correct. But we argue for a more pragmatic approach that builds on the fact that substantial elements of the economies of WTO members could have been labeled as "nonmarket" in the past. Prices were determined by the state, and even today India and Pakistan retain sizeable state-directed price and production rules. One solution for China and other transition economies would be to condition individual sectoral actions on proof that no more than a certain percentage of the total economy is insulated from market forces. For a detailed account of why the bubbles-of-capitalism approach is superior, see Lantz, "The Search for Consistency," pp. 1048ff.

21. Ibid., pp. 1050–54.

22. Constantine Michalopoulos and L. Alan Winters, "Policies on Imports from Economies in Transition: Summary and Overview," in Ehrenhaft, Hindley, Michalopoulos, and Winters, *Policies on Imports from Economies in Transition,* pp. 6–7.

23. Ibid., p.12.

24. Mastel, *Antidumping Laws and the U.S. Economy,* p. 122.

25. Tang Xiaobing, "China's Economic System and Its New Role in the World Economy," in Frederick M. Abbott, ed., *China in the World Trading System: Defining Principles of Engagement* (The Hague: Kluwer Law International, 1998), pp. 59–60.

26. Lantz, "Search for Consistency," p. 1049. The authors are aware of a potentially large complication that will ensue if individual companies or whole sectors are found to be "market-driven": that is, they will immediately be subject to countervailing duties law against government subsidies. We do not propose to enter into a long discussion and analysis here; just sketch the issues from U.S. perspective.

As a result of a 1986 federal appeals court decision (*Georgetown Steel Corp. v. United States,* 801 F2d 1308, Fed. Cir., 1986), countervailing duties law does not apply to NMEs. The theory is that it is impossible to calculate individual subsidies in economies where prices and output are administered by central planning. Should the Commerce Department follow the recommendations in this volume, however, companies and sectors from NMEs would be subject to challenges under the existing U.S. countervailing duty (CVD) laws and regulations. A number of issues will then be raised concerning methodology for calculating CVDs for the company or sector. But one overriding question will stand out: How far back in time will the Department of Commerce decide the subsidy has been in operation? This retroactive dating will have a strong influence on the total subsidy calculation. Currently, the Commerce Department has stated that it will make such determinations on a case-by-case basis. Our recommendation would be for Commerce to assume that all subsidies ended with whatever date the economic reforms of an NME were actually put in place. For more details, see Lantz, "Search for Consistency," pp. 1009–30, 1048–67; Horlick and Shuman, "Nonmarket Economy Trends," pp. 807–29; and Joseph P. Hornyak, "The Treatment of Dumped Imports from Nonmarket Economy Countries," *Journal of International Law and Trade,* vol. 15, 1991, pp. 23–43.

27. Jeffrey J. Schott, *The Uruguay Round: An Assessment* (Washington, D.C.: Institute for International Economics Press, 1994); Sylvia Ostry, "The Threat of Managed Trade to Transforming Economies," Occasional Paper 41, Group of Thirty, Washington, D.C., 1993, pp. 20–23. See also Mastel, *Antidumping Laws and the U.S. Economy,* pp. 101–2, for a typical negative assessment of safeguard rules.

28. Protocol, Part I, Article 2, Section D, paragraphs 19A and 19B, p. 9.

29. Protocol, Part I, Sections 19A and 19B.

30. Ostry, "Threat of Managed Trade," p. 9.

31. Claude E. Barfield, "(Mis)managed Trade," in Edward L. Hudgins, ed., *Freedom to Trade: Refuting the New Protectionists* (Washington, D.C.: Cato Institute Press, 1997), pp. 39–47.

32. Mastel, *Antidumping Laws and the U.S. Economy*, pp. 149, 102.

33. Ostry, "Threat of Managed Trade," p. 14.

34. Brian Hindley and Patrick Messerlin, *Antidumping Industrial Policy and What to Do About It* (Washington, D.C.: AEI Press, 1997). See also Brian Hindley, "The Regulation of Imports from Transition Economies by the European Union," in Ehrenhaft, Hindley, Michalopoulos, and Winters, *Policies on Imports from Economies in Transition.*

35. John H. Jackson, *The World Trading System* (Cambridge, Mass.: MIT Press, 1989), pp. 290–91.

36. Ibid, pp. 291–292.

37. Ostry, "Threat of Managed Trade," p. 20.

38. Ibid., pp. 21–22.

CHAPTER 4: TRANSPARENCY AND DUE PROCESS

1. Claude E. Barfield and Mark A. Groombridge, "The Economic Case for Copyright Owner Control over Parallel Imports," *The Journal of World Intellectual Property*, vol. 1, November 1998, p. 909.

2. Sylvia Ostry, "China and the WTO: The Transparency Issue," mimeo, prepared for the China-WTO Accession Project, Washington, D.C., March 5–6, 1998, pp. 10–11.

3. Ibid., p. 14. See also Pitman B. Potter, "China and the WTO: Tensions between Globalization and Local Culture," mimeo, prepared for the China-WTO Accession Project, Washington, D.C., March 5–6, 1998, pp. 3–4.

4. Kenneth Lieberthal, *Governing China* (New York: W.W. Norton & Co., Inc., 1995), p. 169.

5. Sarah Biddulph, "Legal System Transparency and Administrative Reform," mimeo, prepared for the China-WTO Accession Project, Washington, D.C., March 5–6, 1998, pp. 6–7. For other detailed descriptions and theses regarding aspects of the Chinese legal and administrative systems, see the articles in the March 1995 edition of the *China Quarterly*, particularly: Murray Scot Tanner, "How a Bill Becomes Law in China: Stages and Processes in Lawmaking," pp. 39–64; Anthony R. Dicks, "Compartmentalized Law and Judicial Restraint: An Inductive View of Some Jurisdictional Barriers to Reform," pp. 82–109; and Pitman B. Potter, "Foreign Investment Law in the People's Republic of China: Dilemmas of State Control," pp. 155–85.

6. Potter, "Tensions Between Globalization and Local Culture," pp. 8–10.

See also Sally A. Harpole, "Following Through on Arbitration," vol. 25, *China Business Review*, 1998, pp. 33–38. For an exhaustive analysis of commercial dispute resolution in China, see Stanley B. Lubman and Gregory C. Wajnowski, "International Commercial Dispute Resolution in China: A Practical Assessment," *American Review of International Arbitration*, vol. 4, 1993, pp. 107–78.

7. Dicks, "Compartmentalized Law and Judicial Restraint," p. 86

8. Potter, "Tensions Between Globalization and Local Culture," pp. 8–10. And see Alberto Mora, "The Revpower Dispute: China's Breach of the New York Convention?" *Dispute Resolution in the PRC: A Practical Guide to Litigation and Arbitration in China* (Hong Kong, 1995), pp. 151ff.

9. Harpole, "Following Through on Arbitration," p. 33.

10. According to Harpole, CIETAC handles more cases than any other arbitral body in the world: 1,600 in 1996 and 1997. Harpole, "Following Through on Arbitration," p. 33.

11. Protocol, Part I, Article 2, Section C, paragraphs 1, 2, and 3, p.3.

12. Biddulph, "Legal System Transparency," pp. 7–8.

13. Protocol, Part I, Article 2, Section D, p. 3.

14. These issues constitute the themes throughout Biddulph, "Legal System Transparency," and Potter, "Tensions between Globalization and Local Culture."

15. Potter, "Foreign Investment Law in the PRC," pp. 169–70. For more details, see Pitman Potter, "The Administrative Litigation Law of the PRC," in Pitman Potter, ed., *Domestic Law Reform in Post-Mao China* (Armonk, N.Y.: M.E. Sharpe, 1994); and see Biddulph, "Legal System Transparency," pp. 23–24.

16. Biddulph, "Legal System Transparency," pp. 25–26.

17. Robert Herzstein, "A Transition Mechanism: Outline of Questions for Discussion," mimeo, prepared for the China-WTO Accession Project, Washington, D.C., March 5–6, 1998, p. 16.

18. The discussion in this section is based on Peter H. Schuck, *Foundations of Administrative Law* (Oxford: Oxford University Press, 1994), pp. 338–62. For a description of administrative law and procedures in the EU, see T.C. Hartley, *The Foundation of European Community Law*, 2nd edition (Oxford, England: Clarendon Press, 1988), particularly chapters 11, 13, and 15.

19. Schuck, *Foundations of Administrative Law*, p. 345.

20. Pitman B. Potter and Michel Oksenberg, "A Patch of IPR Protection," *China Business Review*, vol. 7, January–February 1999, pp. 10–11.

21. Mark A. Groombridge, "The Political Economy of Intellectual Property Rights in the People's Republic of China," in Clarisa Long, ed., *Intellectual Property Rights in Emerging Markets* (Washington, D.C.: AEI Press, forthcoming). For discussion and analysis of the pros and cons of specialized court systems, see Stephen H. Legomsky, *Specialized Justice: Courts, Administrative Tribunals, and a Cross-National Theory of Specialization* (Oxford, England: Clarendon Press, 1990). See also Harold Bruff, "Specialized Courts in Adminis-

trative Law," *Administrative Law Review*, vol. 43, Summer 1991, pp. 329–66; and Lawrence Baum, "Specializing the Federal Courts: Neutral Reforms or Efforts to Shape Judicial Policy," *Judicature*, vol. 74, 1991, pp. 217–24.

22. Herzstein, "A Transition Mechanism," p. 14.

23. Protocol, Part I, Article 2, Section C, paragraph 1, p. 3.

24. We agree with Herzstein that it is "unlikely that the process of bilateral governmental consultation will provide a satisfactory remedy for most individual situations in which a business feels it has been treated improperly by the Chinese." Herzstein, "A Transition Mechanism," p. 14. But we believe that the Protocol should specifically provide that governments document patterns of abuse through their local commercial representatives. These could form the basis for an Article 19B consultation and suspension of obligations if a satisfactory response were not forthcoming from the Chinese government.

25. Daniel H. Rosen, *Behind the Open Door: Foreign Enterprises in the Chinese Marketplace* (Washington, D.C.: Institute for International Economics and Council on Foreign Relations, 1999), pp. 242–44 and 252–56.

26. Ibid., p. 254.

CHAPTER 5: PROPOSED REVIEW MECHANISM

1. As quoted in Donald B. Kessing, *Improving Trade Policy Reviews in the World Trade Organization* (Washington, D.C.: Institute for International Economics Press, 1998), pp. 5–6.

2. Ibid., chapter 3. For other descriptions and evaluations of the TPRM, see Sven Arndt and Chris Milner, "Editorial Introduction," *The World Economy*, vol. 1, 1995, pp. 1–9. See also Petros Mavroides, "Surveillance Schemes: The GATT's New Trade Policy Review Mechanism," *Michigan Journal of International Law*, vol. 13, 1992, pp. 374–414; and Aasif H. Qureshi, "The Trade Policy Review Mechanism," in *The World Trade Organization: Implementing International Trade Norms* (Manchester, England: Manchester University Press, 1996).

3. Kessing, *Improving Trade Policy Reviews*, pp. 16–23.

4. Ibid., p. 149.

5. Ibid., chapter 5.

6. See, for instance, the evaluation of TPRM reviews in "Global Trade Policy: 1996," *The World Economy*, 1996, pp. 67–166.

7. Our proposals here are similar to an earlier recommendation presented by Sylvia Ostry in "The Threat of Managed Trade to Transforming Economies," Occasional Paper 41, Group of Thirty, Washington, D.C., 1993, pp. 17–20.

CHAPTER 6: CONCLUSIONS

1. Zhang Shangtang, "*Xishou waishang touzi, jiajie gaizao guoyou qiye*," *Guanli xiandaihua*, vol. 77, February 1995, p. 4.

2. Mark Groombridge, "Dragon Droop: Why China's Economic Future May Not Be as Prosperous as You Think," *The American Enterprise*, July/August 1998, pp. 34–39.

3. Wen Hai, "The WTO and China's Objectives as a World Trading Power," in James A. Dorn, ed., *China in the New Millennium* (Washington, D.C.: Cato Institute Press, 1998), p. 177.

4. Douglass C. North and Robert Thomas, *The Rise of the Western World: A New Economic History* (Cambridge, Mass.: Cambridge University Press, 1973), pp. 1–3.

5. Ibid., p. 157.

6. Greg Mastel, "How to Deal with China," *Journal of Commerce*, July 16, 1998, p. A9.

7. John H. Jackson, *The World Trading System* (Cambridge, Mass.: The MIT Press, 1989), p. 290.

虎

Index

Information from notes or tables is indicated by "n" or "t" following the page number.

—————————— 虎 ——————————

About the Authors

MARK A. GROOMBRIDGE is a research fellow in the Center for Trade Policy Studies at the Cato Institute. Before joining Cato, Mr. Groombridge was the Abramson Research Fellow and the associate director of Asian Studies at the American Enterprise Institute. In addition to his work on Asia, he has written widely on international trade law, intellectual property, and trade-in-services. He has taught at both George Washington University and Columbia University, where he received his Ph.D. in political science in 1998.

CLAUDE E. BARFIELD is a resident scholar at the American Enterprise Institute and the director of its Trade and Technology Policy Studies. He has taught at Yale University, George Washington University, and the University of Munich. He is the author of numerous articles and books, including *Science for the Twenty-first Century* (AEI Press, 1997) and *Electronic Commerce and the World Trading System* (AEI Press, forthcoming).

A Note on the Book

This book was edited by Cheryl Weissman
of the publications staff of the
American Enterprise Institute.
The index was prepared by Lee Brower.
The text was set in Bodoni Book.
Coghill Composition Company
of Richmond, Virginia, set the type, and
Edwards Brothers of Lillington, North Carolina, printed and
bound the book, using permanent
acid-free paper.

The AEI Press is the publisher for the American Enterprise Institute for Public Policy Research, 1150 17th Street, N.W., Washington, D.C. 20036; *Christopher DeMuth*, publisher; *James Morris*, director; *Ann Petty*, editor; *Leigh Tripoli*, editor; *Cheryl Weissman*, editor; *Kenneth Krattenmaker*, art director and production manager; *Jean-Marie Navetta*, production assistant.